I0621958

SONGS ABOUT
SELF-DEFENSE

ALSO BY JOSHUA CROCKER

One Day I'll Know

Snippets of Ink

SONGS ABOUT
SELF-DEFENSE

Joshua Crocker

SONGS ABOUT SELF-DEFENSE

Copyright © 2023 by Joshua Crocker. All rights reserved. No portion of this book may be reproduced in any form without written permission from the publisher or author, except as permitted by U.S. copyright law.

979-8-9879131-2-3 (paperback)

Library of Congress Control Number: 2023918794

Cover design by Joshua Crocker.

Photos courtesy of Integrity Martial Arts.

Classic version, paperback print. First edition 2023.

Published by the Paragon Coalition.
Norman, OK
paragoncoalition.com

Dedicated to my mom, Kevin, and Dan:
Great teachers, leaders, and people.

- - - - - - - -

Foreword by Debra Holmes

I started my martial arts journey over 30 years ago. Through the decades I've been privileged to train with accomplished practitioners. Since 2017 I've been training/working with Joshua Crocker, a talented martial artist, and a personable, innovative, natural instructor.

One more accolade to add to his long list of accomplishments and attributes is being an author. In this book of poems, songs, and short stories, you will find inspiration and a deep heartfelt love of martial arts. For martial artists, young and senior, these writings will give meaning to what we so often feel; yet sometimes can't express. And, for those who are non-martial artists these inspiring and sometimes humorous words will help you understand the martial artist in your life.

Debra Holmes,
Integrity Martial Arts,
Women's Kickboxing and Self-Defense Lead Instructor,
5th Degree Black Belt

"Self-defense is taking the punch.
Ready to fight back, ready to stand up.
Let's keep singing, stayin' alive.
Keep reading, smilin' all the time.
These are songs about self-defense,
they're songs for you. Let's keep fighting."

-   Joshua Crocker

My Training Notes

- Stories About Martial Arts starts on page 1

- The Fundamentals starts on page 39

- What Is the Best Kick? starts on page 77

- I'm Not a Sensei starts on page 113

- The Integrity Collection starts on page 151

- Way of the Samurai starts on page 173

- A Very, Merry Kick-mas starts on page 195

- The Cooler Karate Kid starts on page 231

- Self-Defense Class starts on page 277

Martial Arts Terms

Belt – martial artists wear belts as a part of their uniform, starting as a white belt and advancing to black belt over years of training.

Bunkai – application of moves and techniques from a kata. Commonly done as a set sequence between two or more martial artists.

Bo Staff – a melee weapon with Japanese origins, is a long two-handed stick.

Dojo – a building or home for learning and meditation, typically used in the context of training in the martial arts.

Escrima (aka Kali) – a melee weapon with Filipino origins, is a short stick that may also be used to train strikes with knives or blades.

Gi – a martial artist's uniform.

Grappling – a term used for close combat, including aspects such as striking with elbows/knees, throws/takedowns/sweeps, submissions/chokes, and rolling/wrestling.

Jiu-Jitsu – a style of martial arts with Japanese origins, focuses on close combat, grappling, and takedowns. A popular subset of jiu-jitsu has grown from Brazilian origins.

Judo – a style of martial arts with Japanese origins, focuses on throwing, pinning, or choking an opponent.

Karate – a style of martial arts with Chinese and Japanese origins, focuses on empty hand combat.

Kata (aka Form) – a set sequence and pattern of martial art movements and techniques.

Kickboxing – a style of martial arts with a higher western influence. Sometimes referred to in a broader sense to include any styles of fighting with punches and kicks.

Kyai – the sound you make when striking, often written as the onomatopoeia, "hi-ya."

Katana – a melee weapon with Japanese origins, is a sword with a curved, single-edged blade.

Ninja – an agent or mercenary specializing in stealth and martial arts, now a well-known Japanese legend.

Nunchuck – a melee weapon with Japanese origins, two short sticks connected by a chain or rope.

Sais – a melee weapon with Japanese origins, has a sharp metal prong and two curved prongs on the side.

Samurai – a warrior held in high esteem and nobility. During much of Japanese history, these highly-trained soldiers were military members often equipped with weapons.

Sensei – a teacher or master. Could also refer to an instructor, artist, or professional.

Shuriken (aka Throwing Star) – a ranged weapon with Japanese origins, may take multiple shapes, is used as a metal projectile.

Sparring (aka Kumite) – freeform or focused training used in many styles of martial arts and combat sports. Two fighters will fight in a controlled manner using techniques known to them. With rules and judging implemented, is commonly used for sport purposes in many martial art styles.

Tae Kwon Do – a style of martial arts with Korean origins, focuses on empty hand combat with extra emphasis on kicking.

Stories About Martial Arts
Chapter 1

EVERYONE

Self-defense is for everyone,
because we all have the right to stay safe.
Not a day should go by where that's not the case.
Self-defense is for everyone,
because your rights should be protected,
and your life you should be able to protect,
after all, it's uniquely precious.

You can train whether you're 4, 14, or 40,
you could even be 3 billion-years-old
like my instructor always claimed to be.
Age shouldn't be a measure against you,
why wouldn't you deserve to feel safe?

I'm small and skinny, and frankly not that strong.
But when faced with my side kick,
everyone takes a step back from it.
The size of you isn't near as important
as the size of your dedication and grit.
Don't get down and think you can't hack it,
in the end a punch to the face is a punch to the face,
no matter the size of the arm behind it.

Diversity is a core part of community,
and this dojo is a place where we all train.
We all have our own journey ahead, just think of all
the different colors of belts training under one roof.

We run around barefoot in a gi
with a multi-colored array of ranks,
from beginners to black belts.
It doesn't matter who you are,
we all have a common goal:
to train, to stay safe, to be a part of this place.
And that's something we all share.

The only person I won't train
is a person only out to hurt another.
Danger lurks around every corner,
and danger doesn't discriminate,
the need for defense stems from hate,
so stay safe. Don't be afraid, be proud, be ready.

Man or woman, boy or girl,
you all should feel protected in this world.
Black or white, Asian or Mexican, you all belong.
Be yourself, confident and encouraged
by the colors you wear on your wrist,
whether you're queer, trans, straight, or cis.
On these mats we're all just martial artists.
In this world we're all just people.

If anyone ever tells you that
you don't belong on these mats,
then they're just another reason
you should keep training.
Self-defense is for everyone. That includes you.

PLAYING GUITAR IN GI

Key of A Major, gi of a fighter.
Playing guitar while kicking you.
Da-hm-la-e-oh.
Switching between gis, red, black, and white.
Singing off key, la-de-da-oh-ahhh!
Playing guitar in gi, playing in key.
Singing while swinging my fist.
Da-hm-la-e-oh.
Strike a chord, dunm!
Strike a board, hi-ya!
A martial artist with a song.
A musical artist kicking along.
Da-hm-la-e-oh.
Playing guitar in gi.
Key of G, singing hits.
Play with rhythm and flow.
Fight on the beat.
Da-hm-la-e-oh.
Singing in the key of gi.

5 -- STORIES ABOUT MARTIAL ARTS

MUSIC ABOUT PUNCHING PEOPLE
A GENRE-BREAKING SONG BY JOSHUA CROCKER

Why isn't there more music about punching people?
A chorus to jam out to while you're kicking.
We need lyrics about sparring and board breaking.
Why isn't there a song about punching people?
It's about time someone did something about that.

Yooo! Hit 'em with the hook!
Oh, it's a love song about karate,
singin' rock 'n' roll during a free roll.
A bridge to the next kick!
Oh, it's a pop hit about getting knocked in the head,
singin' country tunes to the tune of a takedown.

Add unnecessary rapping parts,
about the intricacies of martial arts.
Kyai, I say hi-ya.
I'll make you tap when I rap.
I'm closing the gap, roll and trap.
Take the fight to the back alley,
count my fists on tally, beat a boxer from Cali.
Kyai, I say hi-ya.
I'm tough one-upper, keep yo' hands up slugger,
or you'll be just another bruised sucker.
Take a painful hit from my shameful wit.
So get grit, don't omit this submit.

Hit 'em with the hook!
Oh, it's a love song about karate,
singin' rock 'n' roll during a free roll.
A bridge to the next kick!
Oh, it's a pop hit about getting knocked in the head,
singin' country tunes to the tune of a takedown.

Uaaaah-ghgaa-ugghah!
What we need is a punk anthem,
for all those kids who were outcasts in school,
you know who I'm talking about!
The weirdos, the rejects. The bullied infants!
Rise up against the system,
with a swift uppercut followed by a knee strike.
Punch the bag! Punch the government man!
Ugh mom, these neon pink punching gloves
aren't a phase; I need them for bag work!
We're so emo cool, with our gis and black belts.
Ninjas were the original punk icon,
all black from head to toe, (fight on!)
playing the drums with escrima sticks. (right on!)

Hit 'em with the hook!
Oh, it's a love song about karate,
singin' rock 'n' roll during a free roll.
A bridge to the next kick!
Oh, it's a pop hit about getting knocked in the head,
singin' country tunes to the tune of a takedown.

Hey baby, I'll kick you!
I'll do a kata, maybe add a jump kick,
and my footwork is kinda quick!
I'll do a kata, maybe add a jump kick,
and my footwork is kinda quick!
I've gone from white belt, now a green belt.
Green to purple, purple to brown!
Oh, ohh, ohhh! Hey baby, I'll kick you!
I'll do a kata, maybe add a jump kick,
and my footwork is kinda quick!
I'll do a kata, maybe add a jump kick,
and my footwork is kinda quick!
Oh, ohh, ohhh! I've got you in my heart,
and baby, the time we spend apart is the worst.
So... I'll do a kata, maybe add a jump kick,
and my footwork is kinda quick!
I'll do a kata, maybe add a jump kick,
and my footwork is kinda quick!
Oh, ohh, ohhh! Hey baby, I'll kick you!

ROLL WITH THE PUNCHES

You think you can stop every hit?
Really. Yeah sure, I've seen your blocks.
You'll crumble if there's any oomph behind that punch.
You want to learn self-defense, right?
Do you think that means you'll be able
to defend against every bad thing?
I'm a black belt, not Wolverine.

"Oh, it's too violent sweetie."
Boo-hoo, give me a break.
What do you all even think martial arts is?
I've been punched. A lot.
If you don't want to take a hit then take up crochet.
It's a pretty cool hobby.
You don't learn martial arts to never be hit.
You learn martial arts to roll with the punches.
We've got to keep rolling.

The best way to learn to keep your guard up
is to get punched in the face. (Maybe a few times)
Trust me, you're going to learn more,
so much more, from the hits you don't stop
than the ones that you do block.
We've got to keep rolling.

You aren't going to stop every strike.
Whether you're on the mats or out in the world,
there's always another punch waiting for you,
and it'll kiss you goodnight. Sweet dreams.
Roll with the punches, learn how to take a hit.
The mats are a place to feel safe
even with a fist in your face.
Not every shot has to be a knockout.
We've got to keep rolling.

Bruises heal. Fear just gets worst.
You're right sweetie, martial arts is violent.
Life's violent and mean-spirited.
Hateful and unfair. It doesn't take a fist fight,
to lose the feeling of love and care.
You're going to have days and weeks
where you feel weak.
Months and years rid of cheer.
But you've got to keep going.
Learn to take the bad and find the good.
You can't defend against every bad thing.
You just simply can't. Take the hit. Then get up again.
And again. And again. And again. Hit life back.
Punch harder then you ever thought you could.
We've got to keep rolling.

Self-defense is taking the punch,
knowing you can stand up again,
and then hitting back twice as hard.
Keep rolling with the punches.
We've got to keep rolling.

WHITE BELT

A guy named Bob threw a punch,
he wanted to learn karate, a little tae kwon do,
not to mention aikido, jiu-jitsu, and judo too.
He was just a white belt when
he lined up to kick the bag,
stubbed his toe on his first try.
But he kept trying,
learned to kick better,
he has a wicked round kick now.
So he lined up again,
stared down that old bag, his current enemy,
the one he wanted to knock down.
He kicked the bag as hard as he could.
It barely moved.
But he learned a lesson,
one that would be important for him.
He learned how great it is to learn,
that it's okay to try again.
So he kept lining up, knowing one day
he will be able to knock down that bag.

GET READY

Who is it kicking your way?
He's got a smile,
he just ran a mile,
and he fights with style.
Get ready to meet me.
I'm a fighter. I'm a writer.
I'll throw a jab, jab, cross.
I love to hit with a backfist.
I love to rhyme with a list.
Oh-oh, get ready to meet me.
I'm a fighter. I'm a writer.
I can kick twenty times.
I'll jump high and cartwheel around.
I like saying things that sound profound.
Oh-oh, get ready to meet me.
I'm a fighter. I'm a writer.
A black belt and teacher.
A poet and singer.
I love snark, irony, and a zinger.
Oh-oh, get ready to meet me.
I'm an artist with my fists.
I'm a warrior with my words.
So, get ready.

MATS

I step on the mats.
The world is a dangerous place.
But here, I feel safe.
All I have to worry about is
getting punched in the face.
But here, someone helps you back up.
I can put it all behind me.
Learn something, better myself.
And here, as I step on these mats,
I know I'm safe.

SCRAPED KNEE

Have you ever scraped your knee?
A trip left a scrape.
Then you asked for a bandage.
Asked politely.
It hurts a little, stings for a while.
Have you had someone lean down next to you?
Grab a cloth, clean the cut.
Water the blood like a flower.
And the water stings just as much.
Have you cried while they clean it up?
Like the blood on your knee.
The tears on your cheek.
It just hurts, you're just a little embarrassed.
Just a little sad.
Have you had someone tell you it will be okay?
It's just a little scrape.
Nothing more, nothing less.
But you're tough.
They remind you of that.
And you stand up.
A bandage on your knee.
A little hurt, a little sad.
But just as tough.

DON'T FORGET TO BE AWESOME

You don't need me to say this,
but I will anyway.
You're awesome, so cool,
and you're going to blow the world away.
Every day you're going
to make this town a better place,
just by being yourself.
Be kind, the world needs it,
be a leader, live like every day is important.

You don't need me to say this,
but I will anyway.
You're awesome, so cool,
and you're going to blow the world away.
I see someone who has what it takes,
to be so fantastically great.
And just in case you need a reminder,
I know you're incredible, because I've seen it before.
You're uniquely you and uniquely amazing.

You don't need me to say this,
but I will anyway.
Don't forget to be awesome every day!

CHI POWER
A MYSTIC FIGHT SONG BY JOSHUA CROCKER

Channel your chi.
Ancient traditions.
The mystic strike
of the ninja knight.
Ai! Channel your chi!

Focus your energy young one,
imagine your enemy in front of you.
Feel the spirit of your ancestors,
they'll comfort you along the way.
Now close your eyes...
Ow! Someone just hit me.

Channel your chi.
Ancient traditions.
Words of the masters,
heed my advice
if you want to be the karate Christ.
Wait, no. Sorry, that was sorta blasphemous.
Please don't sue me.
Ai! Channel your chi!

This dojo is filled with wisdom,
knowledge is mightier than any sword.
So use this katana to cut these books;
it's a part of your training or something.
Let the wisdom and clarity in,
be enlightened by the ancient presence,
while I go pay the electrical bill.

Channel your chi.
Ancient traditions.
The mystic strike
of the ninja knight,
train when it's bright,
meditate all night,
let the winds take flight.
Ai! Channel your chi!

Now you must wash my car,
it will teach you patience and trust.
Keep your guard up,
both mentally and physically.
A warrior must not be manipulated.
And when you're done with my car,
go paint the fence.
It will aid your evasion skills.
Trust the journey,
don't question the ways of the master.

Channel your chi.
Ancient traditions.
Unlock the dragon's gaze,
trap enemies in a misty haze,
take them out with the wind's force.
Feel the air bend to your might.
Ai! Channel your chi!

Battle your past my gakusei,
don't let the ghosts haunt you.
In order to receive true power,
you must achieve inner peace.
Empty your mind, let your soul and body
become one, as I recently did.
I became one with the wind,
one in spirit, and one in my relationship.
Now meditate calmly,
let the winds call to you.
I must go make a call myself.

Channel your chi.
Ancient traditions.
Please Ashley, take me back. What I said was wrong.
I didn't mean it, really! She means nothing to me!
Please get back together with me. Don't hang up.
No, please, don't hang up. Ashley, I still love you.
Don't do this, don't do this to me.
I've changed, I'm a different person! Ashley, please...
Ai! Channel your chi!

Balance on top of the bamboo stick,
battle the gust of air, stand swift.
You must be blind to risk, be bamboo brisk.
A warrior must be healthy and active,
so stand perfectly still for two hours.
Ignite the flame inside of you,
this is the only way to be a true fighter.
And if you do all this...
next week I will teach you how to punch.
You'll just make a fist, and I guess hit them?
Yes, yes, that sounds right. Ai!

Channel your chi.
Ancient traditions.
Guide the storm,
feel the power.
The mystic strike
of the ninja knight.
The mystic light
of the warrior's rite.
Aaaiiii-ya! Channel your chi!

A NUN WITH A NUNCHUCK

Don't be startled.
She's like a ninja in all black.
Sneaky and mean, she'll attack.
It's a nun with a nunchuck.
Na-na-na-na-nunchuck!

She tells you not to frown.
You'll be the one praying
when she strikes you down.
It's a nun with a nunchuck.
Na-na-na-na-nunchuck!

She's got a spin move that's sinful,
even our kicks won't be a match,
when she hits you upside the head.
Her chain will make us feel the pain.
It's a nun with a nunchuck.
Na-na-na-na-nunchuck!

We have one last Hail Mary,
turn around and fight her with all we got.
But this shall be our last confession,
for she makes no concessions.
It's a nun with a nunchuck.
Na-na-na-na-nunchuck!

"Whenever I tell a joke during a weapons class all I hear are *sais*."

THROWING STAR

A throwing star, shuriken,
and I'm a star throwing a sure thing.
For a throwing star is hittin'
with a throwing star what is hidden.
A shuriken strike, a sort of kin's right,
for a star lighting the night,
is a throwing star, a shuriken right
on the star's targeted flight.

"So, whenever the other kids used to find out I did karate they'd always come and ask me about it. It's always cool to meet someone with similar interests as you. They'd say things like, 'Joshua, I heard you do karate. I bet I could still beat you up. Haha, because you're a small loser. Get it?' Sometimes they would even sarcastically ask me if I would put them in a chokehold or if I could do a takedown on them. Then they would just laugh like they said something super funny. I don't know what's up with that. Any more people just don't talk to me at all. What was my point again?"

SO, YOU KNOW KARATE?

Oooh, I bet you could beat me up.
Let's just ignore the fact you're short.
And you have muscle the size of a grape.
You're also a klutz, and did I mention short?
But la-di-da, you know karate.
How cool is that.
Really though, good for you.
It's good to have hobbies.
Actually this is my-
Can you do a triple jump kick?
Have you ever knocked someone out?
I'm about to.
Haha, don't get too close to me,
I wouldn't want you to hurt me. Jk, dude, jk.
So anyway, what rank are you?
I'm a black belt.
Really? Well, cool.
My step-dad's brother-in-law is a black belt too.
He did like Judo or Kung-Fu or something.
I don't really have the time for that at the moment,
I'm just super busy, but it sounds fun.
Although, I'm worried I might hurt someone.
Haha, that would just be my luck.
Oh, don't worry.
I'm sure you're giving yourself too much credit.

TRAINING

Push-ups, sit-ups, squats.
Stand up and kick.
Sweat drops form on your head.
Keep going, though.
Sometimes training is hard.
The moves are difficult.
The workout is exhausting.
But we train to make ourselves better.
Good things don't always come easy.
But hey, that's what makes it worth it.
When you put in diligent, hard work,
you'll know you earned what you have.
Keep sweating, keep fighting,
and you'll know how strong you are.

"I hated every minute of training, but I said, 'Don't quit. Suffer now and live the rest of your life as a champion.'"

-   *Muhammad Ali*

TESTING NIGHT

Do a kata. Do it again. And again.
Then do eight more katas.
Make your stance wider. Make your kicks stronger.
Make your punches, just better. Seriously.
Fight a black belt. They're well-rested. You're not.
Fight two black belts. They're big. You're not.
Don't stop, definitely don't drop.
It's testing night,
time to put yourself to the test,
and see what you're made of.

WHAT'S YOUR WHY?

"I'm no good at this," Finley said.
I sat down next to them;
this kid was facing the wall,
hugging their own knees.
They wouldn't even look up from the ground.
"What are you talking about?
You're great at this!" I say.
"You're just being nice.
You saw me out there. I'm a failure."
I was about to say something back,
but stopped. They were right.
We sat quietly for a moment
as I thought of what to say.

"Finley, I'm no good at this either.
It feels like I don't have clue what I'm doing.
I still make two or three mistakes every class.
Some days I don't know if I'll ever be 'good.'"
Finley finally turned to look at me.
"They why don't you quit?" they asked.
I think, then say, "Well if I quit I'll never be any good.
I just have to keep trying again and again."

"Yeah, maybe. But you're a black belt.
You are still way better than me."
"Well, duh. But I've had to work hard to get here.
I still work hard, and even now make mistakes.
And still, there is always someone
who I think is better at this than me."
Finley remarked, "So why do you still try?
What if this just isn't for us?"

"Because I want to. I want to know I can stay safe.
I want to improve my body awareness,
and challenge my mental awareness.
And well, I just love doing karate.
This is where my friends and family are.
It's helped me feel more confident.
And now, I love teaching and sharing
that with kids like you. That's why I do this."
As I looked at the student next to me,
I was reminded of all the times I felt like
I was no good and thought I should quit,
but then I remembered why I do this.
I had one more thing to say,
"Finley, why are you doing this?
I love martial arts; this is a part of my life.
How about you? What's your why?"

"I don't know," they said.
"You don't need to tell me now, just think about it."
I stood up and walked back on to the mats.

PURPLE GI
AN INDIE ROCK SONG BY JOSHUA CROCKER

There goes the woman in a purple gi,
she walks by in distasteful confidence.
Her grimace a grin, a kick to the shin.
Her fighting style bruising,
leaving you black and blue.
There goes the woman in a purple gi,
she'll tell you off with a smile,
she'll kick you in the head with style.

She stares at me from across the mats,
asks, "What do you want punk?"
I hate her to her guts and she knows it.
She won't stand around for you to punch,
always complaining when my knuckles nick her.
She knows I'll never beat her in the ring,
her feet are too fast, her hands too quick,
and for me every match is another disgruntled loss.
It drives me crazy the way she walks away after
winning another fight only to turn back and wink.
And it's in this moment,
with anger and frustration rushing through my head,
I know I'm in love with the woman in the purple gi.
And for that reason, I hate her all the more.

The way she stands guard,
stiff and sophisticated like a warrior,
and I swear there is a little death in her eyes.
Quiet pride and false superiority,
until she speaks and somehow it's even worse.
The words from her mouth are bitter,
snarky and strong because she knows she's better.
She can get the best of you with her words,
and I hate how funny it is to her,
the rare laugh she gives
sounds like nails on a chalkboard.

Have you watched closely?
She'll pull her hair back; with the
deadly focus of an assassin she attacks.
Each strike is purposeful, beautiful.
She has the elegance of a tiger and a witch
mixed in one. Her happiness to me is a sin.
And what more can I say,
it's as if one replaced all her grace with hate.

The woman in a purple gi steps into the ring,
knowing she can win against me. It's every time.
She knows I fight worse when angry,
yet she still can get under my skin, my pale frailties.
And she'll complain if she doesn't get her way.
She trash talks and brags after every defeat,
reminding me how much better
the woman in a purple gi is than me.

There she goes,
another man she snaps into a wrist lock,
it's effortless, perfection is everything to her,
forgoing the hard work I spent just to be here.
By principle I never wish to hear
her speak to me again, but every
conversation reminds me how friendly she is,
despite her endless antagonizing.
How can a demon be so enchanting?
I don't know if I want to be her or kiss her,
but I do know I absolutely hate her.

The confidence in every step beknown
to sense of calm ease in her stoic nature.
Swift and angered, she speaks poignantly.
Her kata dignified of everything I hate.
The way she balances infinitely under the pressure
of every kick, snaps every stance into neat succession,
presently strikes seamlessly
with the shouts of sadistic praise.
And in the end she'll bow to endless praise.
Everyone else is mesmerized by her sense of worth,
the havoc of her perfect, meticulous destruction.
As she finishes another show of self-perfection,
I say self-obsession, she turns around and
smirks at me before blowing a kiss my way.
I'm in love with the woman in a purple gi.
The way she speaks, the way she walks, and her
endless fighting to prove she's better than me.

There goes the woman in a purple gi,
she walks by in distasteful confidence.
Her grimace a grin, a kick to the shin.
Her fighting style bruising,
leaving you black and blue.
There goes the woman in a purple gi,
she'll tell you off with a smile,
she'll kick you in the head with style.

It's in everything she does.
Hatred, perfection, obsession.
She's who I can never be,
and at the same time, just like me.
There she goes.
The woman in a purple gi walks by.
I hate her so much.
She'll tell you off with a smile,
she'll kick you in the head with style.
Another man falls to her takedown,
another of her kicks graciously floats to my head.
The woman in a purple gi takes a knee.
Her grimace a grin, a kick to the shin.
As she walks away, her lips glow, her words sting.
The kiss she blew strikes me down again,
and for this reason I now know,
I'm in love with the woman in a purple gi.

The Fundamentals
Chapter 2

ALL THE BASIC RELEASES

They grab your wrist on the same side,
carry the plate and get back with haste.
On the cross side throw a pie in their face
like you're a kid on Kick-mas day.
Two on one, give them a quick stun.
Two on two, throw this book at them for fun.
From behind, boogie and dance,
step on their foot just by chance.
A front choke, lock it down, give them a quick poke.
They grab the back, raise your arm, give them a smack.
Around the neck for a headlock, just breath,
then hit their face, find your base,
make some space, and you'll be able escape.
On the ground you can trap and roll, for sure.
Take control, pin the leg, and hip up.
Same deal if they've got your arms,
just climb the tree and you'll be free.
On your side, take them for a ride,
their head like a picture on the wall, framed.
And finally, when walking through the forest
you get a hug from a bear; you need to be aware.
Elbow like a cat, squat like a chicken, hook the leg,
and once they let go, you scurry like a rat.
Oh and of course, you'll need to yell: "GET BACK!"

THE GRAPPLING RULE

They say space is escape,
so hold your partner near,
like a five-year-old and her teddy bear.

Contact is control,
so pinch your elbows in,
keep your head close and their head even closer.

JAB, CROSS

Jab, cross.
Jab, jab, cross.
Jab, jab, jab, cross.
Jab, cross, squash.
Front leg front kick, jab, cross.
Round kick, backfist, cross.
Jab. Jab. Jab.
Hook, hook.
Jab, cross, hook, hook.
Jab, cross, squash, hook, hook.
Front kick, round kick, elbow, elbow.
Jab, cross, elbow, elbow.
Jab. Jab. Jab.
Jab, cross, elbow, elbow, knee, knee.
Jab, cross, elbow, elbow, knee, knee, guillotine.
Jab, uppercut, hook.
Hook kick, round kick, side kick.
Jab, cross, front kick, backfist, hook, round kick.
Jab, cross, squash, uppercut, crescent kick, side kick.
Front kick, blade kick, side kick, round kick.
Jab. Jab. Jab.
Front kick, round kick, backfist, cross, squash.
Front kick, round kick, jab, cross, squash,
hook, hook, elbow, elbow, knee, knee, guillotine.
Jab, cross.

SMILE

When you don't know what to do: smile.
Nervous or excited, or maybe both,
show it with a smile.
When something's new, it can be scary,
but a smile is the greatest bravery.
So, when in doubt, just smile.

"What do you call a black belt who's hobbies are training with weapons and gardening?"

"A bo-tanist."

4 WAYS

The 4 ways to generate power:

Momentum – The act of moving forward,
by focusing your energy in one direction,
your strike will then have a better connection,
and upon impact has more built-up power.

Rotation – A circle is stronger than a line,
if you can add rotation in any form or device,
you'll increase the curve on thrown strikes;
the hips are the pivot point for your entire body.

Push-Pull – For every action an opposite reaction,
on any strike if you emphasize the pull back
your push out will reflect that upon attack,
therefore the return on a hit is of equal importance.

Penetration – Your power will only go as far as you,
you must go past or through a desired target
or on impact all force will disperse and derogate,
so if your goal is to hit harder, hit farther.

ONE MORE STEP
A RUNNING-PLAYLIST SONG BY JOSHUA CROCKER

You've got your earbud in the left ear,
breathing heavy with a stitch in your side.
Keep running, it's the feeling to stay alive.
In the race you're racing you've got one competitor,
they're behind you poking you with a stick
and in front of you taunting with their tongue out.
You just want to give up
and walk the rest of the way,
but you tell yourself one more step.

Just take one more step,
the finish line is so close.
One more step, one more step.
Say it to yourself, a reminder you've got this.
One more step, one more step.
Breath in, breath out, sing yourself a song.
One more step, one more step.

Tie up those laces and take ten paces,
then take another ten each way.
You'll tire physically before you give out mentally,
it's just running. You'll get there eventually.
'Cardio keeps the cat alive,' you think.
That's a saying right?

Like a time trial, you race against the
ghost from the past, the last time you ran.
Forget the other people on this track,
I'll make it one second faster than the
last time I put on my running shoes.
I'm keeping up with my health,
trying to improve my own success.
So when it feels like my lungs are dying,
remember the wind against your face,
and the satisfaction to feel alive.

Just take one more step,
the finish line is so close.
One more step, one more step.
Say it to yourself, a reminder you've got this.
One more step, one more step.
Breath in, breath out, sing yourself a song.
One more step, one more step.

Apply sunscreen, eat a healthy cuisine,
let's go for a run. It'll be fun, they say.
Race a friend, the winner won't matter,
it's just better to face a challenge with another.
The only person you need to beat
is yourself from yesterday's race.
You've got this buddy!
Don't stop now, make us proud!

The runner's saga, I'd rather be punching something.
Why do people like running?
The feeling to stay alive, to feel your might.
Just keep jogging, keep the pace of the race,
take this life one step at a time.
The hardest things we do make us stronger too.
You're breathing heavy, but you're still breathing,
and that's what this is about.

Just take one more step,
the finish line is so close.
One more step, one more step.
Say it to yourself, a reminder you've got this.
One more step, one more step.
Breath in, breath out, sing yourself a song.
One more step, one more step.

Down the street, feel the fresh summer air.
It's ninety degrees out, the sun's heartbeat beats.
When running in humidity,
you'll learn to find humility.
Turn into the neighborhood,
hide in the shadows of the trees.
But with every step, you're proving to yourself
you're stronger than you thought you were.

The cars drive by; exhaust spouting out.
What are we doing? Why is running so great?
Race past the 7-Eleven, turn the corner.
It's in the final stretch we can catch it.
When you feel like the pain has gotten
the better of you, just tell yourself:
One more step. Just one more.

Just take one more step,
the finish line is so close.
One more step, one more step.
Say it to yourself, a reminder you've got this.
One more step, one more step.
Breath in, breath out, sing yourself a song.
One more step, one more step.
You've got this. Keep running.
Because when you feel weak,
every footstep reminds you how strong you can be.

The air against your face, the feeling to stay alive.

YELLOW BELT

A new day with the sunny shine of Mr. Sun.
Bob had earned his yellow belt
and was ready to keep punching.
He found out that there's more to a punch
then just hitting them real hard.
He learned how to aim his knuckles
so that the bad guy's nose would go *kanuckle*.
He kept his elbow in,
threw a punch with his hips,
and went with the flow.
With a one-two hit,
he was learning what it took to punch.
Never did he think where your feet are
would matter so much for hitting with a fist.
Some fancy footwork,
a lean and a misdirect,
and Bob was starting to land some solid hits.
It's just a hunch, but I'd say he has a good punch.

"What is a feline from New York's favorite thing about martial arts?"

"*Cat-a.*"

KATA MEMORIZATION 101

You're trying to learn a new kata, aren't you?
Well boy, do I've got the program for you.
Welcome to Kata Memorization 101.

Lesson 1: Repetition
Practice each day.
Not for long, but consistency is key.
15-20 minutes is enough time to remind,
and eventually you'll have it down like a rhyme.

Lesson 2: Association
Associate the moves with mnemonic phrases,
storytelling, catchy catchphrases, and color-coding.
Give the techniques another meaning
and you'll find it aids in memorization.

Lesson 3: Chunking
Break the kata into pieces.
Most katas have 5-7 sequences,
practice them one at a time, like pieces of a pie,
then add them together for a delicious treat.

A KNIGHT'S ADVENTURE

Where's my bow at?
Open the door, step through. *(Open guard)*
Look on the floor. *(Step, punch) (Repeat)*

There it is!
Draw the string, *(Low block)*
aim toward the sky, *(Aim)*
and let the three arrows fly. *(Step, punch x3)*

What's that sound!?
Look around, *(Look)*
the ninjas are sneaking in. *(Step around)*
Close the door please, *(Close guard)*
make the last one sneeze. *(Step, punch) (Repeat)*

Let's regroup and defend.
Pick up your arrows, *(Low block)*
drop in the quiver's hold. *(High block)*
Take up your shield, be bold! *(Step, frame x3)*

I hear footsteps...
Look around, *(Look)*
once more the ninjas are found. *(Step around)*
Strike them with the sword you chose, *(Knife hand)*
finish them with a hit to the nose! *(Step, punch) (Repeat)*

Kyai! Achoo!

THE FRENCH REVOLUTION

Se soulever! Allons-y!
The solution to our defense
is a revolution like the French!
Bring out the guillotines,
draw your swords, feel our might!
Drape your arms around their neck,
grab hold of your own hand tight.
Stand strong revolutionaries, hold your base.
Draw your elbows in, be it the blade of the guillotine!
We'll eat that cake now; today our glory shall be seen!
Liberté, egalité, fraternité,
this is a revolution!

AMERICANA

"Keylock, I tap," I said,
though I knew she was sweeping.
I'm rolling and submitting and my elbow pries.
Counting the spots from the side mount position.
Shoulder trapped in a lock of America.
Trapped in a lock of America.
Trapped in a lock of America.

STRIKEOUT

Up by one in top of the ninth.
Two outs, bases loaded, the home crowd cheers.
You're on the mound,
a baseball bat in their hands.
A roundhouse is your curveball.
Snap that bat in half.
Don't let them run home.
Here's my tips:

Step to the side,
position yourself through the target,
for extra momentum and penetration.
STRIKE ONE!
Stir the pot, build up extra energy,
throw your arms like a pitcher,
so you may use your whole body.
STRIKE TWO!
Hit with your shin, tomorrow it will bruise,
right on the grip of the bat,
and be sure to kyai loud on attack.
STRIKE THREE!

MY SIDEKICK

On every mission he's right there for me.
When tyranny is on justice's footstep,
my sidekick will always come through.
He is the one who stops evil in their tracks,
levies the tension with a quip,
knocks through the enemy's guard,
always listed right under my name in the credits,
with knockout looks (but not in an intrusive way,
like I'm still clearly the star, but you'll be thinking,
oh that main hero guy, he has a pretty cool sidekick),
he'll use his heel to cure and heal any catastrophes.
For every hero in the spotlight,
there's a sidekick helping save the day.

"I've heard some people say they wish they felt safer while driving. I get it, you can't use traditional martial arts training to stay safe behind the wheel. You just need to remember to be calm, stay aware of your surroundings, be patient, and if you're still nervous, have you considered studying in the ancient art of *car-ate*?"

FIGHT TO FIGHT ANOTHER DAY

Fight to fight another day.
Live and run away.
Don't let pride stop you from losing,
because there will be some fights you can't win.

You can train for years,
learn all the self-defense you can,
but the best thing I can teach you
is to know when to wave the white flag.
When it comes to your safety
and the safety of others,
there are no winners.
Just people who don't lose.

So, fight to fight another day.
Live and run away.
Don't let pride stop you from staying safe,
because there will be some fights you can't win.

DON'T BE STUPID

Don't be stupid, be safe.
If something sounds dangerous,
then maybe, just maybe, don't do it.
Don't be stupid.
I like music and podcasts and I pretend
to like audio books to sound smart,
but if I'm walking around without the ability to hear,
then I can't really be aware, and it'll be much
worse when no one can hear you screaming.
Don't be stupid.
If someone seems sketchy, they might be.
If something feels wrong, it might be.
If somewhere looks creepy, maybe stay away.
Intuition is a gift, use it.
I'd rather be wrong than get hurt, or worse.
Don't be stupid.
It's not scary. It's not that hard.
Lock your car, keep your eyes open, be cautious,
when you're alert you don't need to be scared.
Keep your head clear.
Be aware.
Don't be stupid, be safe.

LOUD

A RAP ROCK SONG BY JOSHUA CROCKER

Be loud, grab their attention.
Speak up, speak your mind.
Can you hear me yet?
I said be loud, grab their attention.
Speak up, speak your mind.
I'm shouting out for crying out loud.
I said be loud, loud, loud!
Don't back down, shout a little louder.

Let's lower it back to room temp.
Here's the problem for you,
you're walking around in the dark,
looking around, thinking this is snark,
but when you meet my pain,
you'll be hitting the floor soon.

So don't freeze, don't wait,
instead fight back like you know to do.
And like my music blaring now,
be the fire in the concert hall,
make security evacuate that place,
but they'll be stuck watching in awe.

Get back from me! I said stay the y'know it, away!

Be loud, grab their attention.
Speak up, speak your mind.
Can you hear me yet?
I said be loud, grab their attention.
Speak up, speak your mind.
I'm shouting out for crying out loud.
I said be loud, loud, loud!
Don't back down, shout a little louder.

When you're outmatched physically,
entirely in the dark mentally,
why will you stay so quiet?
Make them pay attention to you,
ask for some help and scream the threat,
get the mob to make 'em repay the debt.

Because let's get real for a second,
no one has any right to mess with you,
they should keep their face away,
before they face my fists when you shout out.
And that's just it, yell, scratch, and claw until you
bloody that nose they should have kept to themselves.

Get back from me! I said stay the y'know it, away!

Be loud, grab their attention.
Speak up, speak your mind.
Can you hear me yet?
I said be loud, grab their attention.
Speak up, speak your mind.
I'm shouting out for crying out loud.
I said be loud, loud, loud!
Don't back down, shout a little louder.

And don't think you can keep
the perversion in a form of tears,
because when you're lying just to weep,
do you think this is the time to lie low?
No, you've got to start speaking,
and let that caring bystander in to help.

This problem won't just affect you,
if you let the mugger on the loose,
let your self-destructive thoughts choose,
you're going to let that hurt you too?
Slander and crime rise in your own head,
shout 'get back', let your support back in.

Get back from me! I said stay the y'know it, away!

Be loud, grab their attention.
Speak up, speak your mind.
Can you hear me yet?
I said be loud, grab their attention.
Speak up, speak your mind.
I'm shouting out for crying out loud.
I said be loud, loud, loud!
Don't back down, shout a little louder.

When society wants a nice new toy for their box,
speak up, let them know what's up when
they mess with us. Shout out, be loud!

Don't grab me! You're hurting me!
I said get back!

In the alleyways and no-more safe places,
yell your rights, tell them to keep their hands
in their pockets, or sock 'em. Shout out, be loud!

Don't touch me! I don't even know you!
I said stay the y'know it, away!

If you're struggling inside looking
for a reassurance of something calm,
then find your friend, and quietly ask for help.
Ask for love. Even the smallest of cries, can be
a sound loud enough. So shout out and be loud.

DROP THE BEAT

Drop the beat, here we go.
You throw, the blow, punch at me,
it's a punch I see, punch please.
In and out, throw and shout,
out and in, back again,
here we go again!
Oh, the blow, I'll throw,
punch, stun, have fun,
inside, gut punch, inside toss,
lift and walk, grab and toss,
wrap, lift in, senagi throw, ya loss.
In and out, throw and shout,
out and in, back again,
here we go again!
Oh, the blow, I'll throw,
punch, guts, ribs, I rib, kidney,
take a knee, stomp the knee,
outside, side strike, outside sweep,
shoulder seize, back leg sweep,
grab and drop, dump, ya weep.
Oh, drop the beat, drop your feet,
in and out, out and in, a throw down,
meet the ground, hit the pit, take the floor,
add a finish, you're finished, and the song is finished!

THE BEST STYLE

What is the best style of martial arts?
Tae Kwon Do is kicking its way in.
Karate with its strikes and weapons.
Jiu-Jitsu rolls and throws, tap or snap.
Kung-Fu has enlightened, fast strikes.
Judo tossing everything around, don't choke now.
Kickboxing for an attack, footwork to counter back.
Aikido controls the fight, controls the enemy.
Muay Thai hits hard and doesn't care what's fair.
Krav Maga diffuses the threat, wins the fight.

Truthfully, each style has something great.
I would say the best style is situational.
But the worst style is whichever one you do.
Yeah, there I said it.

ALL THE SAME

There's like, over 150 styles of martial arts.
And whenever you talk to someone who
has never done martial arts, only seen it on TV,
they'll be like, "Oh, karate and jiu-jitsu.
Those are pretty much the same thing, right?"
Yeah, sure. They're completely oblivious.

But once you start to research or train,
you see the important differences.
Each style is unique and different.
And just assuming otherwise
is ignorant and disrespectful.

And now I've been training in
the martial arts for years, over half my life.
I've trained in multiple styles and met masters
of different backgrounds and experiences.
I've researched and learned more about martial arts,
seen and trained all these different styles,
and I've come to the conclusion,
that in the end, they really are all the same.

I mean, a punch to the face is a punch to the face.

PUNCHING POEM

Performing punching prescribes particular pieces.
Please prepare proper provisions precisely.
Perhaps, prerequisite playing premises.
Pin palm, point punching parts.
Picture partner's pompous, pretentious plan.
Payback perversion, prevent panic progressing.
Preserve peremptory peace.
Progress punch pressure precisely,
persistently pitching pain.
Physics plays part powering punch;
push punch perfectly, paving pain's path,
penetrate past people's practicality,
prepare pulling punch performance.
Paint perfect picture, polish pace.
Parting punching platitudes:
Primary perceptions, practice persistence.
Physically pack power,
prepare possibly painful premise,
primarily pausing people's putrid peccability.
Pow!

HANDS UP

Here's a cool sparring trick:
Keep your hands up.

What Is the Best Kick?
Chapter 3

INSTRUCTION MANUAL: FRONT KICK

The Ap Chagi, the Mae Geri.
A beginner's favorite, the base of all kicks.
There's three kinds of front kicks.
Snap, thrust, push. Alright, enough.
Let's get started.

Snap kick:
Hit with the ball of your foot.
Whip your foot out, your rechamber is key,
because a snap kick needs a good pull back.

Thrust kick:
The in-between, still hit with the ball.
Engage your hips, thrusting them forward
to get a more targeted push through on your kick.
This kick has both the whip of the snap kick,
while also having the momentum of the push kick.

Push kick:
This time chamber higher and kick with your heel,
not a very quick kick in comparison,
but this one has the most power. You'll stomp
through your target to knock them back.

79 -- WHAT IS THE BEST KICK?

INSTRUCTION MANUAL: SIDE KICK

The Yeop Chagi, the Yoko Geri.
Plenty of power, a great stopping strike,
the side kick is not the sidekick in this story,
but the main hero of kicks.

Hit with your heel, knock them back.
Stomp through your target.
Spin your chamber around to build power,
then fire it right back at them.
If they've got you on the ropes,
Plant your base foot and just fire a side kick
right into any advancing adversary.

The Japanese use it a bit differently,
what I call the blade kick.
Hit with the side of your foot
and flick your foot under someone's guard
or right at that knee they use to stand.
A more niche use of the kick
that may not knock someone back,
but it is a bit faster, with a sorta sneaky streak.

INSTRUCTION MANUAL: ROUND KICK

The Dollyo Chagi, the Mawashi Geri.
The kick of all targets, the round kick.
Kick them in the head,
kick them in the knee.
Kick them in the side,
kick them wherever you please.

Rather than using your foot,
you'll make contact with the base of your shin.
First point your knee at your target,
this is the chamber.
Flick your foot out, kick with the shin as discussed,
and you got a wicked kick to hit with.

You can fire a round kick quick,
and with balance can do it over and over again
without sitting your foot down,
all the while switching your targets.
It makes for a very versatile and useful kick.

FOUR PARTS

Balance on one foot,
chamber for your kick.
Send your leg out,
hit with a stomp or flick.
Rechamber afterwards,
stand stout like a wall of brick.
Finally sit your foot down,
and get ready for your next trick.

THUNDEROUS I

The days were getting shorter.
Our hopes were getting darker.
It was back in the days of war.
I was younger, but my hair was gray.
We showered in our own tears.
The roses were dying. Entropy, I say!
The darkness was upon us...
"Surprise!" Then we flipped the lights on.
Presents, balloons, birthday cake.
Hey, there's always time for a party.
I tend to exaggerate and fabricate stories.

But truth be told, we were at war.
The dojo was under siege and things
were more dire than they've ever been.
I was our newest black belt and I
wanted to prove myself to the team.
So one day I spent the afternoon in the dojo library.
I was trying to find a way, any way we could win,
end this war and train in peace again.
I learned about a kick so powerful it could
knock back an entire class. Take out any blight.
Few had ever mastered this move,
but I knew it was up to me to learn,
the Thunder Kick. *Ba-ba-bum*

INSTRUCTION MANUAL: BACK KICK

The Dwit Chagi, the Ushiro Geri.
Do you like donkeys? Donkies? Donki?
No I was right the first time.
Anyway, meet the donkey kick, the back kick!

Look over your shoulder,
please always look.
Then scrape your kicking leg right by your base leg
and then back your back kick right into them.
This kick is a lot like the side kick, use your heel,
but this time point your toes down.
This kick will swing up after a minimal chamber.
Great way to get a hit or stop in
from an otherwise difficult position.

"Do you know what you do when you get kicked? You kick back."

CRANE KICK

This is a poem I call, 'Crane Kick.'

Da-da-da-doo-oh-ah-eh-da-da-doo-oh!
Hi-ya!
Da-da-da-doo-oh-ah-eh-da-da-doo-oh!
Hi-ya!
Da-da-da-doo-oh-ah-eh-da-da-doo-oh!
Crane kicks are stupid!

Thank you for your time.

CRANE KICK II

This is a poem I call, 'Crane Kick II.'

Da-da-da-doo-oh-ah-eh-da-da-doo-oh!
I was a little harsh before.
Da-da-da-doo-oh-ah-eh-da-da-doo-oh!
To amend my last poem,
I will admit they do still look a *little* cool.
Da-da-da-doo-oh-ah-eh-da-da-doo-oh!
They're just impractical.
And kinda stupid.

Well more like, really stupid.

INSTRUCTION MANUAL: CRESCENT KICK

The Bandal Chagi, the Mikazuki Geri.
The kick of circles. In and out. Out and in.
As elegant as the night's moon, the crescent kick.

Unless you're incredibly flexible,
this kick isn't best utilized for striking,
but a great setup kick (or just a good stretch).
You can either go in to out, or out to in.
Lift your leg up and circle it around.
Open up your hips to get a full extension.
You can knock your opponent's guard down,
then hit them in the head.
Or simply use all that momentum to
build up for an even stronger second kick.

INSTRUCTION MANUAL: AXE KICK

The Naeryeo Chagi, the Kakato Otoshi Geri.
Chop! If a tree fell in the forest...
Chop! Plop! Split a log quick with the axe kick.

The crescent kick's outdoorsy sister.
The two kicks start the same,
can be done in to out or out to in,
but the axe kick drops in the middle.
Chop! Make the bad guy's collarbone go 'plop!'
When your foot is at its apex,
pull it down and hit with the back of your heel.
Split the wood in two.
Break the board in half.
Chop! Chop! Chop!

THUNDEROUS II

I had the book on the mats sitting near me and
two notebooks filled with messy handwriting
propped open right next to it.
I was determined to master the Thunder Kick.
I had been practicing in the corner by myself,
my friends were all practicing bo techniques.
We had heard a rumor that the defection dojo
were planning an attack this weekend.

Stomp, kick, turn, jump, ah, lost my balance.
The kick was challenging.
First, you had to stomp your heel
at just the right angle.
Then a fast kick, almost side kick-like.
Quickly after you do a three-sixty turn and jump,
throw your heel around at their head, and finish
by pulling your opposite shin down for a kick.
And at the very end you must give
an earth-shattering kyai.
I've never believed in any of that
martial arts mysticism, but that kyai,
there was something different about it.
A certain energy to it,
I just couldn't seem to replicate.
Regardless, I kept practicing. I had hope.
We all had hope. We had to have hope.

TRAMPOLINE

Let's bounce!
Just the two of us,
me and my kick.
They think I'm done,
but this next trick
will be pretty sick.
I'll sit my foot down,
and bounce!
Kick 'em again,
quick hit for the win.
Up and down,
bounce around,
kick 'em once,
sit my foot in front,
they'll be enticed,
so I'll kick 'em twice.
Let's bounce!
B-b-bounce!

"What would it like to be transported to a cartoon world? Maybe one with anthropomorphic animals where you have to use your martial arts training to win the big kickboxing tournament. You battle your way up the ranks, and finally it's the grand championship. You can't lay an egg in this match or it's all over. Your opponent is a semi-aquatic mammal, a dangerous foe with venomous ankle spurs. Quite a good kicker, I imagine. If you were to ask me how to defend against the potentially fatal kick of your opponent, my advice would simply be to parry the platypus."

95 -- WHAT IS THE BEST KICK?

INSTRUCTION MANUAL: HOOK KICK

The Huryeo Chagi, the Ura Mawashi Geri.
Like a fish in the water, they'll take the bait,
and get caught on my hook. Just you wait.
The hook kick, don't get got.

Raise your foot to kick,
and oh, no, you missed!
But that's just it.
After you kick, you'll just hook it in.
And before your opponent knows what hit 'em,
they've got a concussion and twenty to life.
Hit with your heel, some call it the heel kick,
the two are nearly the same.
Knock 'em in the head, rock 'em to bed.
And like a fish to the bait,
they'll get got when they're caught.
Caught right on the hook kick shot.

INSTRUCTION MANUAL: TWIST KICK

The Bituro Chagi, the Uchi Haisoku Geri.
The twist kick is just sick.
Misdirect what they expect.
Mate, this kick is metal.
Ay, twist your leg like a pretzel.

Chamber like any other kick,
they're ready for a front kick,
but bam! Snuck around their guard real slick.
Plot twist! Don't be salty,
I hope you got your popcorn and pretzel,
cause this movie just got real interesting.
From your chamber, twist your foot to the inside,
then flick your foot out for a kick.
The twist kick is a versatile misdirect,
you can hit them in the gut, head, or inside thigh.
Not only that, but with the twist,
you can hit them where they expect a fist.
In close or far out,
the twist kick will hit you no matter what.
Just hit with the ball of your foot
or pull your toes back and hit with the top,
just depends on the target and distance.
The kick will work either way,
and they'll never see the plot twist coming!

ORANGE BELT

Throw a punch, time to dodge.
Bob has his gloves on, kicking boots strapped,
headgear protecting his sculpted jaw.
Move to the left, throw a hook to the right.
More fancy footwork and a quick jab here.
He's sparring as an orange belt now.
With the basics of how to punch and kick down,
he's become quite a decent fighter.
Quite the warrior some may say,
but this is the day he met another challenge.
Another sparrer a tad bit better, kicked his butt, er,
and he fell down to the ground.
But he stood back up and kept fighting.
Bob knew no matter how dire things seemed,
if he could just keep moving,
things would be okay.
And for now, keep moving he did.

"I fear not the man who has practiced 10,000 kicks once, but I fear the man who has practiced one kick 10,000 times."

-    *Bruce Lee*

THUNDEROUS III

The sky was cloudy. A storm was on the way.
We've been through storms countless times,
but this one would bring the enemy with it.
I remember clearly, it was a Saturday afternoon.
The defectors had a strike planned.
The last time we fought them, they ambushed us.
We were weakened, and honestly we still
hadn't recovered. But we couldn't let them win,
or our cause would be a lost one.
And you should know this about the defection dojo,
they used their martial arts for evil.
And they wouldn't stop until they won.
So it was our job to make sure they lost for good.

All it would take is one kick,
I just had to pull off the Thunder Kick one time.
I had gotten close a few times,
but close wasn't good enough.
All it would take is one kick,
no one has ever done it twice in a row.
No one has ever needed to; the Thunder Kick was
the kind of kick that could end a fight instantly.
Stomp, kick quick, turn, jump, heel, pull down,
and kya- whope! I slipped right at the end.
I picked myself up. Time to try again.

101 -- WHAT IS THE BEST KICK?

BUTTERFLIES

She gives me butterflies.
My breath is taken away momentarily.
Two crescents of the moon intersect,
a beauty unknown to the world.
Two skips in my heartbeat.

I'm met with a knockout shot of adrenaline
as I walk her way to say the word hi.
The thought of her drifts in the air,
the way she gives me butterflies.

"Why does martial arts give you confidence? Well, it lets you – no matter who you are – become the strongest version of yourself. You can feel safe even in fear. And if anyone ever gets in your way, you know you can kick them in the head."

KICK LIKE A GIRL
A PUNK-ROCK SONG BY JOSHUA CROCKER

"You fight scrappy, kid!" Buzz off, I'll end you loser.
Duck and run, I'm here for the fun.
Smile more, doll. I'll sock you in the jaw.
Do you think we would make a good team?
Burn the town down.
She's a high kicker, I'm an elbow smasher.
She's a leader and teacher, I'm a statistician thinker.
I want to kick like a girl.
I want to kick like her.
Kick like the world's a theater on fire.
She's a strong fighter, a pretty little liar.
A dream wrapped in a katana blade.
I want to kick like a girl.
I want to kick like her.

Woah-oh-oh-oh! I want to kick like a girl.
Kick a man in the head.
Make everyone's jaw drop when
they see my kicks keep the beat.
The prettiest kicks you've seen.
The nastiest hit you'll take.
Woah-oh-oh-oh! I want to kick like a girl.
Kick like a girl. Kick like a girl.
Woah-oh-oh-oh! I want to kick like a girl
Kick like a girl. Kick like a girl.

Put your speech on hold preacherman,
one question can derail your whole class.
Amelia will pilot your jet to the sky.
The way you whip your kicks like that.
You can hear the wind snap and sing.
I wish I could sing like that; I sound like a boar.
Am I a bore? She's another awesome person.
I've got my friends, amazing women I know.
Watch a kicking show unfold.
A butterfly kick floating midair.
Watch her footwork dazzle and explode.
A tornado kick breaking ribs.
I want to kick just like that.

Woah-oh-oh-oh! I want to kick like a girl.
Kick a man in the head.
Make everyone's jaw drop when
they see my kicks keep the beat.
The prettiest kicks you've seen.
The nastiest hit you'll take.
Woah-oh-oh-oh! I want to kick like a girl.
Kick like a girl. Kick like a girl.
Woah-oh-oh-oh! I want to kick like a girl
Kick like a girl. Kick like a girl.

Where I'm from ladies aren't allowed to speak;
I think it's time we stand-up to the bullies.
When I was growing up boys couldn't wear pink;
I think it's time we roundhouse the bad guy's face.
She can hip toss a mobster, fight demon monsters.
Can I have that jacket sleeve, please?
You're so freaking cool.
You've broken boards with a hit from your thigh.
Lady, how do you kick like an angel and samurai?
Never tell her how I look up to her and her words.
Don't let her know I can't really sing,
I'm faking it till I'm making it great.
And I'll kick just like that.

Woooaaahhh-ahhh!
I want to kick like a girl!
Make the whole world hurl!
We'll keep training, growing stronger.
Welcome to the new world,
where everyone can be a great fighter.
I want to kick like a girl!
My dear, clutch your pearls!
Welcome to my foot,
it tastes like soot.
I want to kick like, I want to kick like,
I want to kick like her.
I'll spin and twirl, swirl and whirl!
And kick like a girl!

Woah-oh-oh-oh! I want to kick like a girl.
Kick a man in the head.
Make everyone's jaw drop when
they see my kicks keep the beat.
The prettiest kicks you've seen.
The nastiest hit you'll take.
Woah-oh-oh-oh! I want to kick like...
Woah-oh-oh-oh! I want to kick like....
I want to kick like a girl.
Woah-oh-oh-oh! I want to kick like a girl.
Kick like a girl. Kick like a girl.
Woah-oh-oh-oh! I want to kick like a girl
Kick like a girl. Kick like a girl.

Woah-oh-oh-oh! I want to kick like a girl.
Like a girl. Like a girl. Watch out world.
Woah-oh-oh-oh! I want to kick like a girl
Like a girl. Like a girl. Watch out world.
I want to kick like her. Kick like a girl.

THUNDEROUS IV

"Places!" shouted one of the black belts.
To the left we had students with bo staffs and sais,
to the right our best at takedowns,
in the middle the towering fighters,
and by the back door were the grapplers
just in case they sent a few to sneak in the back.
Crackle-boom! The rain had started pouring.
The enemy arrived with a bang.
We were expecting a battalion of martial artists,
but we never imagined just how many there was.
Crackle-boom! A flash of lightning lit the sky.
The fight was on! Our best fighters went at it.
Kevin was quick to take down a few
high ranking fighters, Dan took on the
enemy sensei in a fierce clash of bo staffs.
Bridgette led our forces in perfect formation,
even Bob had gotten in on the fight. Just one
punch from Bob is enough to take out most people.

Crackle-boom!
We were holding our own,
but the defectors were starting to wear us down.
A few of their black belts and brown belts
had broken our ranks.
Instantly, we knew what they were after.
The blade.

Crackle-boom!
I was the last student in the way.
Admittedly, I was cowering in the back.
I had tried the Thunder Kick earlier but failed.
I fell backward and took a bit of a beating after.
But I knew this was our chance.
I stepped back into a sparring guard.
Stomp.
Quick kick.
Turn.
Jump.
Hit with the heel.
Pull down my shin.
Crackle-boom!
Aii-yaahh!
The opponent in front of me was knocked down.
Then, I did it again.
Crackle-boom!
And again.
Crackle-boom!

This was our chance.
Our dojo fought with all we had,
and we won.
From that point forward,
things started looking up for us,
and it wouldn't be long until the war was over.
Or so the story goes.

"Most of the stories in this book are true. There's a lot of sound advice throughout the pages. But the legend of the Thunder Kick, to this day many don't believe it ever happened. As the days of war have become more hazy in my mind, I myself am not sure any of it ever happened. But what is a legend but a dream. A hope of what can be done."

WHAT IS THE BEST KICK?

The best kick hits hard.
The best kick is quick.
It's flashy, but practical.
It's elegant, but powerful.
The best kick is the one you practice
over and over until you've made it perfect.
And once it's perfect,
you find a way to make it better.
Front kick, side kick, round kick, back kick.
The best kick is filled with confidence.
Crecent, axe, hook, and twist.
The best kick doesn't miss.
You don't need to be flexible.
You don't need to be tall.
You don't need to be the strongest.
If you practice a kick,
it can still be the best one.
Because the best kick
is the one you'll invest in.

I'm Not a Sensei

Chapter 4

PRINTER

Being a martial arts instructor
sounds like such a cool job:
fighting other black belts, teaching ancient moves,
and apparently trying to fix this gosh darn printer!
I just need to print a test prep sheet;
why won't this thing work?

The life of a martial artist is often romanticized;
all the kicks, breaking a wooden board with ease,
and having to replace the paper in the paper tray,
because *someone* forgot to reload it after last time,
and that *someone* was probably me.
Oh great, and now we're out of cardstock. Just great.

My students think I can do a triple jump 360° kick,
knock over a bag with my fist,
win the grand champion trophy at every tournament,
but what I can't do is print the flyer for the
tournament because the printer ran out of ink.
So now I have to check the
mailbox daily for our ink delivery.

Being a martial arts instructor takes
the discipline of a statue, the confidence of a lion,
and the patience of someone using a printer.

THE FIRST CLASS I TAUGHT

Charyut! Alright class, let's get started.
Today we will be learning how to kick.
So first you have to bring your knee up…
That looks great Teddyroy!
He says to the stuffed bear lying on the floor.

Here, Peter, try to break this board.
He grabs the stuffed doll's hand and punches the board with it. He then proceeds to try and break the board over his knee, taking an embarrassing amount of attempts before it finally breaks.

Add a punch after your kick now Sammie.
This time he's talking to his four-year-old sister.
Do it just like this. *He shows her how to punch.*
At least she's a real person. And nowadays she's a black belt. So the first student I ever taught is a black belt now. Take that every martial arts master ever.

Baro! Great, let's get started on our first form.
Let me just turn on some music first.
He runs over to a blue radio and plays a CD from the TV show, Phineas and Ferb. Which is an amazing show by the way. And the songs are absolute bangers. Okay aside over, let's get back to class.

Alright, first you're going to turn left and low block…

WHEN I ACTUALLY STARTED TEACHING

Break! Our next drill is going to focus on combos.
You want to start with a front kick, then jab, cross.
We call this a kick, punch, punch combo.
By starting with a kick you can close the gap and...
...uh...
...umm... *(say something)*
...ah, uh... *(close the gap and...)*
...uhh... *(I don't know what to say)*
...ugg, um... *(they're all staring at you)*
...ahm... *(just say something already!)*
...ah, uh... *(it's been nearly ten seconds now)*
...uhhhh... *(why is it dead quiet in here)*
...um... *(would anyone notice if I just ran out the door)*
...uh... *(I wonder how much a ticket to Mexico costs)*

Here, let me just start over. So you see, combos.
And kick, punch, punch, and yeah that's it.
Let's get started y'all! *(I nailed it)*

FREAKIN' GREAT

There's nothing I'll tell you to do,
that I'm not willing to do too.
If you keep trying, you're going to be great.
C'mon give me a little credit as a teacher.
You all should believe in yourself,
cause I believe in you.
It's my responsibility to make you shine.
Are you willing to keep giving your best?
I'll push you further, pull you up,
and one day you'll be even better than me.
That's my goal for each of you.
And just know, you'll all be so freakin' great.

FAVORITE WORD

Everyone has words they love.
The words autumn, ocean, and midnight.
Labyrinth, mystery, and enigma.
Aurora, magenta, and indigo.
What's your favorite word?
A hard consonant with a soft vowel,
a smooth transition of syllables,
a sharp sound on the tip of your tongue.
I can say with a fair amount of confidence,
that everyone's favorite word is a simple one:
their name.
Learn and remember someone's name.
It's the simplest way to get to know someone,
and build a connection with them.
Given, chosen, taken, a name gives meaning,
and each of us give our names meaning.

Although everyone's second favorite
word should be, "Onomatopoeia."
It's an objectively great word.

YOU DON'T SAY
AN ALTERNATIVE ROCK SONG BY JOSHUA CROCKER

I can sell the world.
I'm the feature on a hit record.
I won the champion belt in seven seconds.
And best of all I'm a martial arts teacher.

You don't say, you don't say.
Hey, hey, hey. *You don't say.*
And hey, it's a brand new day.
You don't say, you don't say.
Hey, hey, hey. *You don't say.*

I can sell the world.
I can sell Brooklyn Bridge.
Make a rich man beg.
I can end a world war with a word.
I can make a drop of blood look like a drop of gold.
And I can take these words and tell a story.
A generational visionary, a new missionary,
Jesus loved the world, that's what I heard.
Oh hey, but you don't say...
You don't say, you don't say.
Hey, hey, hey. *You don't say.*
And hey, it's a brand new day.
You don't say, you don't say.
Hey, hey, hey. *You don't say.*

I'm the feature on a hit record.
I'm the lyrical wonderkid.
A song stuck in your head.
I can move a mountain to tears.
I can make the beat repeat endlessly.
And I'll create a world with a thought.
A new voice fought, in everything I've taught,
my life's a musical, a beat acoustical.
Oh hey, but you don't say...
You don't say, you don't say.
Hey, hey, hey. *You don't say.*
And hey, it's a brand new day.
You don't say, you don't say.
Hey, hey, hey. *You don't say.*

I won the champion belt in seven seconds.
I won your heart in a monsoon.
Make a tall man small.
I can break a wall with a whisper.
I can take an army in an hour.
And you'll fall in love with me in a glance,
let love and war take chance, I fight with a dance,
I'll punch the abyss, my fist's a first kiss.
Oh hey, but you don't say...
You don't say, you don't say.
Hey, hey, hey. *You don't say.*
And hey, it's a brand new day.
You don't say, you don't say.
Hey, hey, hey. *You don't say.*

And best of all I'm a martial arts teacher.
I know tae kwon do.
I teach karate, be a kicking literati.
Take on the world with a word.
Be great, learning is a mystery. Something new
is learning history. Learning, a victory.
And you can light a flame all the same.
Confidence in your name, reignite the game,
kicking down your wall, standing up after the fall.
Oh hey, but you don't say...

You don't say, you don't say.
Hey, hey, hey. *You don't say.*
And hey, it's a brand new day.
You don't say, you don't say.
Hey, hey, hey. *You don't say.*
And hey, the world's okay.
You don't say, you don't say.
Hey, hey, hey. *You don't say.*
And hey, I'm not going away.
You don't say, you don't say.
Hey, hey, hey. *You don't say.*
You don't say, you don't say.
You don't say, you don't say.
Hey, you don't say.

"I didn't win a lot of tournaments growing up. I was a small kid. I didn't practice for competition that much. We've always been a self-defense-based dojo. I only took home gold at one tournament of the dozen or so I went to. But the day I finally went to a tournament as a teacher, with my own students watching from the side, was the day I finally won. And not only that, but the people I helped prepare for this tournament got their own medals too. Sure, you could just say I was a bit older. Finally had a growth spurt. Now I'm just below average height. I simply think every teacher is made better by their students."

MAKING A LIVING KICKING

I make a living kicking.
I always wanted to be a teacher.
Now I get to teach others to kicks.
It's pretty great.
I fight others for fun.
Step in the sparring ring.
I am lucky, I'll be grateful.
I get to do what I love daily.
And I love kicking people.

TIME WELL SPENT

Do what you love.
Spend your time growing up.
Look back and know it was time well spent.
You get one life, make it a great one.
Spend your time training on the mats.
Spend your time singing songs.
Spend your time with family and friends.
Spend your time living.
Don't wait, do what you love.

"If you love life, don't waste time, for time is what life is made up of."

- *Bruce Lee*

LITTLE KIDS

Little kids can't sit still.
They listen by talking.
And they always have to pee.
But they love to learn new things
because to them, the world is there's to explore
and there's so much out there to do.

Little kids will say the craziest things.
They are so confidently incorrect.
And they always have energy.
But at the end of the day they'll give you a hug
and smile no matter how great or bad the day was.
Because you took the time to talk with them.

Little kids want someone to listen to them,
and they'll tell you the sweetest things.
Little kids want to get better at things,
because they want to be like you.
Little kids want to make friends,
because everything is better with a friend.

They're just like us in the end.
And there's plenty we can learn from them.

LIGHTBULB MOMENT

If you want to get better at anything,
try teaching it.
When you teach it makes you think.
If you can make someone else great at something,
then you'll realize how you can make it great.
I've discovered so many things I never knew,
just by explaining it to someone else.
There's a lightbulb moment when you
finally understand what you've been doing.
So, if you want to master something,
if you want to understand something,
if you just want to improve something,
try teaching it.

PORTRAIT

There's the dream of being famous.
I'll make it big someday.
Fan mail pouring in, my portrait everywhere.
The day my words echo louder than they're spoken.

But today, I got handed a drawing.
Scribbles, colors outside the lines,
which is where colors belong if you ask me.
It's a portrait of me, that looks nothing like me.
It's got giant words at the top of the page.
One of the letters is written backwards.

Fame is overrated.
I don't need my own star,
or the appreciation of strangers.
Stranger danger, amiright?
I've already been given plenty of fan mail.
I have several portraits of myself.
They're from my favorite people.
And I'll always be their biggest fan.

DON'T TELL ME WHAT I'M NOT

You remind me I'm not a sensei cause of my ranking.
First off, that's ignorant of the meaning,
it's a Japanese word simply speaking,
denoting a teacher, instructor, artist, or professional.
Last time I checked I'm all those things. Or has my
boss been writing those paychecks just for funsies?
You want to tell me I can't be called a sensei,
because of some ancient tradition (circa the 1980's),
even when I teach people martial arts daily.
And I love to do it. And if I may, I'm pretty good at it.
I know I'm not the most talented martial artist,
and no, I haven't been doing the same dozen katas
for a quarter century. Time well spent I'm sure.
But I know I'm one of the best teachers you will find.
And the team around me are even better.
My teachers are amazing people, sensei or not.
So if you're going to gatekeep your karate techniques,
just know, you'll never be the teacher I am.
That black belt doesn't make you an instructor,
katas, gold medals, degree upon degree
mean nothing when it comes to teaching.
The way you lead, the words you say,
the people you change. That's what matters.
I'm a teacher, instructor, artist, professional,
but I'm not a sensei. Fine then. I'm so much more.

"There's some jerks wearing black belts. Just like anything else in life, martial arts has its bullies and gatekeepers. I've met instructors and senseis who couldn't teach you how to tie your shoes. Sure, they could probably beat me up, but they hoard the knowledge for themselves. I've got one goal as a teacher: make my students better than me. It takes a lot of humility to be a good teacher, and there are plenty of days where I could use a reminder of that. But despite my shortcomings, I know if I can make a difference in at least one person's life, I've done something good. And then I'm going to do it again."

TRADITIONAL DOJO
A SKATE PUNK SONG BY JOSHUA CROCKER

Da-na-da-na-da-na. Da-na-da-na-da-na.
Da-na-da-na-da-na. Da-na-da-na-da-na.

The traditionalist masters are going blind.
They want to keep with the ways of old,
so they can protect their boy's club.
They're egos are so fragile and weak.
Break a toothpick board with a side kick.
Mister, I'll break your face in a second.

Da-na-da-na-da-na. Da-na-da-na-da-na.
Traditionalist bum. You're dumb.
Da-na-da-na-da-na.
Bow again cult-leader.
Worship the ways.
Keep everything the same.
Da-na-da-na-da-na.
Traditionalism is a plague.
Keep blind allegiance.
Fight the paraplegic.
Da-na-da-na-da-na.
Traditional dojo
with cult-like mojo.

Da-na-da-na-da-na. Da-na-da-na-da-na.
Students, bow towards me.
Praise our home, praise our ways.
Brothers and sisters on these mats.
Hold hands, link with your family.
Follow my words, hold my stories in regard.
We're the one way, there's no leaving the fray.

Da-na-da-na-da-na. Da-na-da-na-da-na.
Get out of my way,
you wish you could fight like me.
Keep your loser scrolls, with "ancient words".
A systematic prejudice view of martial arts.
I can do three butterfly kicks in a row,
you're just a sad old man. So old.

Da-na-da-na-da-na. Da-na-da-na-da-na.
Traditionalist bum. You're dumb.
Da-na-da-na-da-na.
Bow again cult-leader.
Worship the ways.
Keep everything the same.
Da-na-da-na-da-na.
Traditionalism is a plague.
Keep blind allegiance.
Fight the paraplegic.
Da-na-da-na-da-na.
Traditional dojo
with cult-like mojo.

Da-na-da-na-da-na. Da-na-da-na-da-na.
Students, bow towards me.
Listen to my legendary stories.
Proverbs of the truth are what I speak.
Fight us in the ring, you must defeat your weakness.
Only through the blood of the battle dome
can you be accepted in our home.

Da-na-da-na-da-na. Da-na-da-na-da-na.
You're a scum predator with a stupid name.
You just sit on your throne; thou are holier than none.
You think only warriors belong to martial arts.
That's code for men with a hefty bank account.
Outsiders should be punished with an iron fist.
Their crime is being weak. And different.

Da-na-da-na-da-na. Da-na-da-na-da-na.
Traditionalist bum. You're dumb.
Da-na-da-na-da-na.
Bow again cult-leader.
Worship the ways.
Keep everything the same.
Da-na-da-na-da-na.
Traditionalism is a plague.
Keep blind allegiance.
Fight the paraplegic.
Da-na-da-na-da-na.
Traditional dojo
with cult-like mojo.

Da-na-da-na-da-na. Da-na-da-na-da-na.
Students, bow towards me.
Recite the chant, pledge allegiance.
Pray for mercy when fighting the enemy.
It's not a cult, we're a congregation of warriors.
A united family with a common vision,
martial arts truth-holders, the greatest fighters.

Da-na-da-na-da-na. Da-na-da-na-da-na.
Da-na-da-na-da-na. Da-na-da-na-da-na.

Traditionalist rat. You're fat.
Traditionalist bile. You're senile.
Traditionalist bum. You're dumb.
Da-na-da-na-da-na.
You're a mockery spouting hypocrisy.
Make martial arts a ruse, cover-up your abuse.
Your dojo is a cult and an insult.
Da-na-da-na-da-na.
Bow again, bow your head,
hopefully you'll soon be dead. You're an old man.
Say worship the ways. Keep everything the same.
Da-na-da-na-da-na.
Traditionalism is a plague. Master. Sensei.
A wrinkly regent. Keep blind allegiance.
Call the other side weak. Fight the paraplegic.
Da-na-da-na-da-na. Da-na-da-na-da-na.
Da-na-da-na-da-na. Da-na-da-na-da-na.
Another traditionalist cult. A fake dojo front.

THE HAVENDRY FAMILY

It's a sad truth. There are bad people in martial arts. I wish I could say otherwise, but as with every group of people, you're going to see some rotten apples. I would like you to meet the Havendry Family.

I've run into the Havendrys on a couple of occasions; they run the local martial arts underworld. They help cover up scandals; they've kept many a shady dojo from closing. Ever heard of the Black Belt Black Market? All of the unsavory weapons and supplies you could need – they'll sell it to you. For a hefty price of course. Illegal fights? They've got you covered. Need to place a hit on someone? Sure thing.

My teacher has a scar across his chest from an encounter with them several years ago. He was trying to stop them from delivering a large supply of weapons to a nearby dojo. This dojo has a reputation of teaching martial arts not for self-defense, but rather violent, vindictive combat. Their students often choose to train at their gym so they can use martial arts to injure or even kill others. I wish martial arts was purely used for self-defense, but with such power there will always be those who abuse it.

My teacher was able to find the spot they had been exchanging the weapons at and took them on head to head. He got cut by one of the knives they had sold. He fortunately was able to win the fight and be delivered to the hospital in time. And in the end several of the instructors from the dojo got arrested. However, the Havendry Family made out without any consequences. They always do. Too often the bad people get off without facing any repercussions, while the good people take the fall. And it's a reality we must accept, as bitter as it may taste.

I've seen the Havendrys help black belts and coaches untangle scandals. It's disgusting what these people who claim to be martial artists have done. Teaching is a privilege, but to these people it's a chance for exploitation. Self-defense is supposed to make people feel safer. Trust me, the victims of these so-called black belts were never safe. It's sickening.

The Havendry Family is a blot on the martial arts community. A crime family who cares more about power than anything else. I say all this not to scare you but remind you. There is evil out there, so be aware. Not everyone has good intentions. But even more so I want to remind you what it means to be a martial artist. Be someone who wants to make the world a safer, better place.

"And a lean, silent figure slowly fades in the gathering darkness, aware at last that in this world, with great power there must also come -- great responsibility!"

-   *Stan Lee, Amazing Fantasy #15*

VIOLENCE

Why is self-defense violent?
Is martial arts evil?
Do the ends justify the means?

Can't we all just stop fighting?
There's always so much fighting.

VIOLENCE II

Why is self-defense violent?
All the punching.
All the kicking.
The takedowns and chokes.
Just remember:
The world is violent too.
There's bad people out there.
There's fighters who want to harm others.
I've said it before, I'll say it again:
The best lesson you can learn
is to get punched in the face.
Make peace with the violence.
Find patience in the chaos.

When you punch a bag,
you learn how strong you are.
When you kick a friend,
you learn how to balance.
And we have to balance the good against the bad.
Remember what it is to be a martial artist.
Remember what self-defense means.
To stay safe against evil.
To feel confident in the world.
To stand up again, even in all the violence.

"The ultimate aim of martial arts is not having to use them."

- *Miyamoto Musashi*

GREEN BELT

Bob is bobbing and weaving.
His green belt swinging on his hip.
He ducks, he jumps, he spins away.
His evasion paired with a slip,
and blocking paired with a parry,
has become quite the obstacle for competitors.
Bob isn't the kind of guy to just let you hit him.
He uses his kicks to keep you away.
His reverse sidekick knocks bags over
in a second now. And a second is all he needs
to knock you to the floor too.
He knows where his feet are will make his punch
all the stronger when it hits you.
He keeps his elbow in, round kicks with the shin,
strikes with a spin of the hips.
Watch out world, cause Bob is starting to get good.
Just how good will he get?

TRY AND STOP ME

Just go ahead, try and stop me.
I'm just going to keep leading,
teaching, speaking.
I'll keep fighting till the world's a better place,
I'll stay on the path till I've won the race.
I won't stay quiet if I shouldn't be,
when I need to listen I'll take a knee.
Because I have a chance to make a change,
so why wouldn't I?
There's a smile on my face, a real one,
there's tape on my belt, truth in my words,
and goodness in the world.
Stand up, stand up for that world.
Stand up, stand up for those who need you to.
Stand up, stand up after you're knocked down.
Let's just do some good.
No matter what, I'll do something good.
Just go ahead, try and stop me.

SUCCESS

Just balance and pull my foot back in, Finley thought.
They picked up their foot and hook kicked the bag.
As they rechambered, Finley lost balance a little.
They stumbled back a step or two.

"Hey, there you go! Great kick Finley," I shout.
Finley walked to the back of the line. *I still lost
my balance. I have to stop tripping at the end.*
Once they got to the front of the line again,
Finley tried the hook kick another time.
They stumbled again, but the kick was still good.
"You're looking pretty good at this kick," I say,
"What do you think of the hook kick so far?"
"I really like the kick; I just wish
I had better balance," they say.
"Well, just really focus on your base leg. And if you
work on keeping your hands closer in, that may
help. Balance takes times, just take it slow and keep
practicing. You'll get there before you know it."
"Okay, I'll try that. I have to make sure I do my best."
"Do you like this kick?" I ask. "Yes," they say.
"Have you got better at it today?" "Yes."
"Then that's a success," I tell them.
Finley thinks about it then smiles. "You're right.
Today was a success. And I can keep practicing to
make it even stronger."

"We make sacred pact. I promise teach karate to you, you promise learn. I say, you do, no questions."

-   *Mr. Miyagi (Pat Morita)*

STUDENT AND TEACHER

There are no bad students, just bad teachers.
There's a power behind knowledge,
one that may be used for good or evil.
And some days it feel like the evil's winning,
doesn't it?

How do we create the perfect ending?
Too often are things sad and tragic, anti-climactic.
We all can build the world, tell a story with a word.
Just remember it takes more than
only yourself to make a change.

To every leader, lead them the right way.
Center stage, all eyes on you, with the responsibility
to take action, knowing the world can be better.
Each word you say can echo ten times louder.

To every hero, remember the kid who looks up to you.
You may just be you, faults and all,
but to the kid who wants to be you,
you're so much more, success or not.

To every teacher, you can create a world,
and cursed be those who waste that gift,
because the world needs someone good,
and I need – and *we all need* someone
to show us how to create it.

The Integrity Collection
Chapter 5

INVEST IN YOURSELF

It's an investment worth making.
To make the best of yourself.
You can be absolutely great,
and at the least you can be absolutely you.

Now it ain't easy,
but the best things never are.
What is important to you?
Where are your eyes set?
Put in the work and time.
Ten minutes today and every day,
in a year's time you'll see how far you've come,
and in a lifetime you'll see how great you are.
All it takes is an investment,
an investment in you.

NEVER GIVE UP

Don't get down on yourself if you fail the first time.
Or the second time. Or the third time.
Or the hundredth time. Lightbulbs work, don't they?
You want to be great, then what's it going to take?

Never give up, not on your darkest days.
Never give up, even when you fail again and again.
If success was perfection we would all be failures.
Keep trying, keep smiling, keep knowing I'm right there
the whole time. I want you to succeed; do you?
Then keep trying and keep smiling.

Never give up, not on your darkest days.
Never give up, even when you fail again and again.
My friend, this is an investment, it takes time.
We need perseverance; have you looked outside?
Things aren't okay. I'm starting to figure out
they never were and never will be.
But if we give up, then what?
Things will never be the way we want them to be,
but we can learn to thrive against the chaos,
live with a smile instead of hatred and fear.
Never give up, you're going to get punched in the face.
You'll learn to keep your guard up;
you'll learn to punch back.
You want to be great? This is what it's going to take.

TEACH BY EXAMPLE

A leader doesn't shout from the front,
they push from behind and pull others along.
Take example, and lead by example.
Get right in the mix and do your best.

Life's your stage, and all eyes are on you.
Give them the performance of the century,
if they see you they'll have a reason to never give up.

You don't need to be perfect,
you don't need to be an instructor
to teach others by your example.
If you give your best, that's still 100%.
I'll say someone who tries and wants to get better,
is someone worth learning from.
Be it you're five-years-old or five times that,
I see great examples all around me.
The best leaders are the ones
who are always learning.

You never know when someone is watching you.
They see the example you set, the person you are.
Be the person they strive to be.
An example worthing looking up to. That's you.

EARN RESPECT

The golden rule is made of gold.
To treat others the way you want to be treated.
We all want to be treated well,
with love, kindness, and grace.
We all want to be treated like human beings.
So don't chase after riches of gold,
when a drop of respect is all we need.

Respect those above you, so you learn.
Respect those below you, so they grow.
Respect everyone just like you.
Earn respect from yourself,
by being a person you can be proud of.

We all just want respect,
to be treated like we belong.
Don't turn them away,
be the one to open the door,
and you'll earn more than riches.
Show them love. Earn respect.
The golden rule is made of gold.

"I always tell my students that just because I have a black belt doesn't automatically mean I've earned your respect. I have to get up here each day and earn your respect; by teaching you, encouraging you, and helping you whenever you need it. There are people out there who think just because they're a black belt, a teacher, a professor, or any level of master that you should automatically respect them. That's ridiculous. If my students have to earn my respect, then I don't see why I don't have to earn theirs."

GROW WITH YOUR PEERS

It's a lot more fun to train with friends.
I would have quit a long time ago without them.
I'm thinking of the kids I knew when I was young,
the stupid jokes we made in classes.
I'm thinking of the girls, who I'm embarrassed to
admit, got me back to training when I was in a rut.
I'm thinking of the friends who stay late with me
after classes end, to practice and talk for a bit.
I'm thinking of the family who makes being on the
mats more than just training, but a part of my life.

Don't think you've got to grow up alone.
There are other people who are there with you.
Make friends with them, the people around you.
One of my favorite things about life is that
vastly different people can become friends.
So many stories in each of us, and by chance
these are the people who you get to know.
They get to know you and grow with you.

When you spend all class throwing someone
to the ground and then they punch you in the face,
you learn to be friends. It's sorta funny.

Growing and learning are easier
when you don't have to do it alone.

REACH YOUR GOALS

Climb the ladder of success one step at a time.
I didn't earn my black belt overnight.
Take it one day at a time,
reach for the stars one night at a time.

Life was never meant to be a sprint,
because you'll tire out on the side of
the road after a mile. This is a marathon.
Pace yourself, keep a plan for yourself.
What do you want out of life?
Out of this year, this month, today?
Who's going to cheer for you from the side?
You'll need someone to hold you up when
you're out of breath and want to quit.
Set a goal, make it a challenge,
then go out and cross the finish line.
Watch as your fans cheer you on the whole way.
Then get set, because the
second lap is coming up next.

Climb the ladder of success one step at a time.
I didn't write a book overnight.
Take it one chapter at a time,
reach for your pen one page at a time.

"It's a good thing I didn't earn my black belt overnight. Well technically, I did earn my black belt overnight, since the test kept me up to at least 3 a.m. And if you want to talk about running a race, they made us run a 5k before the test even started. And trust me, I learned the hard way you can't sprint through that. If they had let me go for my black belt after only a few months of training I simply wouldn't have made it. I had to take it one step at a time just to get there. And it made earning it all the more meaningful."

"Confidence is an amazing thing. I started martial arts to boost my confidence, and sometimes it seems it worked too well. As long as I don't have to give a sales pitch or talk to that girl I like.

You'd be surprised at how far you can make it on blind confidence alone. Confident people can make competent people second guess themselves. Try walking into any building and just act like you belong there; 90% of the time no one will stop you or bat an eye, even if you've never been there before. Ha, confidence is a dangerous weapon. But if you use it properly, it can be your greatest strength as well."

I WILL SUCCEED

A failure always fails, because that's who they are.
That's why I tell myself I ain't a failure.
I will succeed, achieve all my dreams,
because why not?

Confidence is just past success remembered,
if you got to this point, you've made it this far,
why not go a little farther?
I will succeed, achieve all my dreams,
because why not?

It's not fake it till you make it,
it's keep trying till you've made it.
Tell yourself you believe in yourself,
or else you won't be able to be your best.
Confidence gets you far in life,
inspiration is innovative and motivative,
initiative indicative of success.
Tell yourself I will succeed, I've got this.
Because if you believe in yourself,
greatness is in your sight.
I will succeed, achieve all my dreams,
because why not?

TEST YOUR LIMITS

Let's kick it up a notch!
Carpe diem, seize the day.
Take it to the limit,
take a step into the future.
One foot, one second, one more.
A little better. Just a little better.

Mess around and find out.
Find out where you're at.
Take it to the limit,
then take it just a little farther.
Push yourself to become better.
Turn twenty reps into twenty-two,
and shave a few seconds off your best time.

And just remember:
Life was never meant to be a sprint.
Pace yourself, keep a plan for yourself.
One step at a time, don't go and hurt yourself.

Let's kick it up a notch!
Carpe diem, seize the day.
Take it to the limit,
take a step into the future.
One foot, one second, one more.
A little better. Just a little better.

"Some of the things you learn in martial arts can be uncomfortable or scary. That's why we train. The mats are a place where you can feel comfortable and safe, even when you otherwise wouldn't.

Some of the things you do in martial arts can be challenging or difficult. That's why we train. One piece at a time, one challenge to focus on. If you can make yourself a little better at something, that's a success. Sky's the limit, as long as you keep trying."

YES I CAN!

Shout with me now: Yes I can!
Shout it aloud: Yes I can!
I can, I can, yes I can!

I can stand up again.
I can take another step.
I can speak up against all else.
I can be confident in myself.
I can live with a smile.
I can live without one too.
I can do the best I can.
And yes, I can keep my guard up.

Shout with me now: Yes I can!
Shout it aloud: Yes I can!
I can, I can, yes I can!

BEGINNER'S MIND

Keep a beginner's mind,
always wanting to learn,
to grow and be better.
Look at the world with wonder,
and wonder how you can flounder.
Did you know my black belt
is made of white fabric?
Every time I rip another
thread while training,
I'm reminded I'm still here to learn.
Always keep that spirit,
the mentality of growth,
a curiosity about you,
a beginner's mind.

BLACK BELT BODY

With my black belt body, I'll train.
Let each kick soar to new heights,
every block will knock you back.
Train like an Olympian,
move like a ninja,
fight like a black belt.
I'll do my very best.
And train to make my best even better.
Train my body, my mind, my heart,
to be who I want to be.
It won't be without perseverance and adherence
before I'll reach that appearance.
But no matter who I am, where I am at,
I can train with my black belt body.

WARRIOR'S HEART

There's a leader with the heart of a warrior.
A fighter fighting for what's right.
So tell me, what am I doing tonight?
I want to be a leader, the hero.
The hero, not a zero.
I'm sitting here though.
Do I fight for what's right?
I've made an enemy of my friends.
How do you do it?
Lead with a warrior's heart.
There's a fighter fighting for what's right.
Speak up, speak out, don't speak over.
Smile, cry, don't lie. Fight, be the light.
Compassion in your eyes. Obsession left behind.
Kindness in your voice. Lead by choice.
Fight out of love, not out of anger.
There lies the balance of a friend and fighter.
The one with the heart of a warrior.

The Way of the Samurai
Chapter 6

THE WAY OF THE SAMURAI

An ancient attack,
the way of the samurai.
A code and degree.
Mystic and proud.

The way of the samurai is extinct.

Heroes aren't eternal,
the gods have fallen from Olympus.
The ancient attack is in ruins,
the decree of the elders is broken.
The samurai has been struck,
a warrior lying dead.

All we have now is people,
people trying to save the world.
But these people,
they're not samurai.
They're just people.
The stories aren't in black and white,
they're complex shades of gray.
They don't want to be forgotten.
But just as it was with the way of the samurai,
they'll end up extinct too.

Will the dream of the hero always stay a dream?
Shall it be...

PURPLE BELT

With the fabled war begun,
the story of Bob is far from done.
He's advanced his skill, just earned his purple belt.
The best fighter is one with friends.
Teamwork is the name of the game now,
Bob was a little hesitant to accept that,
but when his teammate took out
the enemy lurking up from behind,
he knew he couldn't fight this fight alone.
Bob became a loyal ally, trusted his team.
He knew they would never betray him.
I remember those days,
I was still a kid when we fought together,
protecting our dojo with dignity.
Even if he still struggled with his katas,
his sparring was a little clunky,
we all knew Bob had the heart of a warrior.
Confident in what he knew, always ready to learn,
and had a passion rare amongst anyone.
He cared for each of us, a team player till the end.

BECOME THE BEST

I'm on a journey to
become the best martial artist ever.
You'll see my kicks on TV at the next Olympics;
taking down Al-Baghdadi and Putin with my fist.
I'm on a journey to
become the best person you know.
You'll hand me a Nobel Peace Prize;
I will cure cancer or maybe solve world hunger.
I'm on a journey to
become the best.
And I won't rest until I'm the greatest ever.

Remember my name.
This is *my* story.

DRESS UP

Superheroes dress up before fighting crime.
Does spandex make you heroic?
Super spies have a whole budget just for sunglasses.
Does a suit and tie make you a better kicker?
Martial artists wear robes and belts.
Does tradition make you a real fighter?

Heroes play dress up.
What are they hiding?
They use martial arts.
What are they fighting?

I'M THE HERO / I CAN SAVE YOU

I'm the hero of the story.
I know I am.
Because if I'm not...
am I really the villain?
...
... no.
... no, I can't be.

I can save you.
I can save the world.
I'll come up with another plan.
Trust me, just hold on a little longer.
I can save you.
I'll love you.
This is my story; I can be great enough.
I'm strong enough to save the world, to save you.
Just hold on a little longer.
I'll save you.
I'm the hero. I'm the-
I'm the...
I'm the hero, right?

I have to be, because if I can't save you,
then I'm a- I'm a failure. And I can't be a failure.
I won't be. I just, I just won't, okay!

I can save you from the pain,
I won't let the world hurt you anymore.
I'm the one who will love you,
I'll be your shining hero.
I'll be your hero; I need to be your hero.
Just hold on a little longer, okay?
I'll catch you.
I can save you.
I'll love you.

I won't let you go, okay? Just, trust me.
I won't lose another friend. I won't lose an-
I won't lose again.
Because I love you. I have to.
And if I can't love you,
then who's going to love m-
who's going to love...

I'm the hero.
I'll prove it.
I just have to save you.
I just have to-
I just...
I just have to make the story mine, okay!
I'll save the day,
because *I'm* the hero.

I need to be the hero.

THE HERO WITH NO POWERS
A SUPER AWESOME COMIC ROCK SONG BY JOSHUA CROCKER

A cape and a mask to hide your anxieties,
a gadget belt to fall back on,
because without it you're nothing.
The hero with no powers,
the hero who uses martial arts to save the day,
because without gimmicks they've got nothing.

Play dress up,
fight evil all you want.
Save the town, get the girl.
Your alias in all the tabloids.
Kids want to be you,
adults are jealous of you.
But, c'mon dude.
What have you really done?

Flying high in the sky, first class.
Punching down walls of paper and glass.
Take down the bad guys, kick... butt.
The hero with no powers.
Kick and punch, fight and fight, jump and leap.
Invisible without the mask. (No one cares)
Invincible because of privilege. (Life's unfair)
The hero with no powers,
climbing skyscrapers one floor at a time.

Your name is on every billboard.
The most popular costume this Halloween.
But is the town any safer now?
You say you're a public savior,
but can you do us all a favor?
Just go away. You're not helping.
We don't need another fixer breaking things,
another hero making things about himself
instead of helping us when we really need it.

Swing by, by grappling hook,
hit the baddies with a wicked right hook.
Your brand and logo on your chest,
be sure the cameras get your good side.
Save the poor family just for the fame.
The streets sing your praise,
but you're as much a menace to us
as deep down you know you are to yourself.

Flying high in the sky, first class.
Punching down walls of paper and glass.
Take down the bad guys, kick... butt.
The hero with no powers.
Kick and punch, fight and fight, jump and leap.
Invisible without the mask. (No one cares)
Invincible because of privilege. (Life's unfair)
The hero with no powers,
climbing skyscrapers one floor at a time.

Catchy name, catchy theme song.
We must stop crime.
Lock everyone up.
Bruise and break the bad guy's face.
You don't apologize for using mace.
You're always right, aren't you?
Vigilante justice expert
and PhD in psychological care
from 'Trust-me-I'm-a-superhero U.'
Dude, you're a narcissist in pajamas.

The friendly neighborhood hero,
shakes your hand on the street,
kisses babies on the cheek,
saves the princess from her castle,
the kind of guy you'd want to grab a beer with.
Are you really a friend to us?
You claim to save the city,
but you make every headline about you.
You're our friend when it's convenient,
the rest of the time you're a Broadway reject.
You're not the hero we deserve.
But you make sure you're the one we need.

Flying high in the sky, first class.
Punching down walls of paper and glass.
Take down the bad guys, kick... butt.
The hero with no powers.
Kick and punch, fight and fight, jump and leap.
Invisible without the mask. (No one cares)
Invincible because of privilege. (Life's unfair)
The hero with no powers,
climbing skyscrapers one floor at a time.

You hide behind a mask, what are you afraid of?
The hero with no powers,
nothing special about them.
Martial arts and gadgets for the rescue.
Do you really want to help make things better?
Or do you just want to feel better about yourself?
This isn't about saving me,
it's about feeling like you're a good guy.
You want to be a hero,
even though you have no powers.
The rest of us will take the fall.
Whatever. I guess this is your story, after all.

LAST ONE STANDING

When I'm the last one standing,
that means everyone else is gone.
I've been fighting, I've been thriving.
Becoming the greatest of all time,
the best version of myself possible.
I'm the last one standing,
and now all my friends are gone.

They've been suffocating in this
burning building, consumed by flames.
I'm on the outside singing like no one's listening.
They're listening. They're crying too.
Never has a dying call been so quiet,
I can't hear them over my own voice,
which it turns out is all I care about.
Don't say I might be selfish. I know I'm selfish.
Self-centered and self-obsessed too.

I'm the last one standing,
everyone else is falling apart.
I look around at the decaying world. What have I done?
Where was I, when everyone else is gone?
I'm the last one standing; I know I'm great.
Joshua, was all this worth it?
Because when they're gone,
you'll know you're nothing at all.

APOLOGIZE

Let go of your pride already.
You know you blew up.
It doesn't matter who's right.
You shouldn't have yelled.
It's okay to admit you made a mistake.
You're not perfect, no one is.
Does being right matter more than
mending a relationship?
No one will think less of you.
And if they do,
that's their problem.
It's okay to apologize.
Even if first, you have to admit to yourself,
you were wrong.

Hey, I'm, uh,
I'm sorry.

DON'T SAY A THING
TAKEN FROM SNIPPETS OF INK

Don't you say a thing,
this is a problem you can't fix.
Just be there. Just listen.
Not every problem has an answer.
Don't you say a thing.
Just be there. Just listen.
Just say you love me,
no matter the pain I'm going through.

"What I should have said is nothing. I want to help others, but what's not my trial I can't fix. Next time let me just say, 'I love you.'

I can't heal the world, no matter how many push-ups I do, I'll never be strong enough. I can't save every damsel in distress, especially when I feel so stressed. What I should have said is nothing. Shut up and listen to you.

I'm sorry I can't keep myself from talking. I'm still working on building my self-control, learning that heroes come from works of fiction for a reason. Next time I'll just say, 'I love you' and listen."

I'M NOT THE HERO

I'm not the hero of the story.
I'm just me.
And I'm trying to remember that.
I don't need to save you.
I just- I just...
I just want to be your friend.
And I may not have any superpowers,
but I'll still love you till the end.

I'll be a hero in the small ways.
I'll be the hero who really does love you.
I'll be a friend.

"In pitch black skies, a candlelight shines brighter. When darkness is around, a spark fills the room."

THE WAY OF THE SAMURAI II

The way of the samurai returns.
There's a hero inside of us,
but we must do what's right.

At the dinner table,
dismiss bigotry.

Mind other's space by
keeping your hands to yourself.

Don't be okay with hate
when you can call it out.

Apologize,
even if it hurts.

When it's not your story,
be a part of the supporting cast.

Be aware,
when dangers lurks near.

And listen,
when all someone needs is love.

A Very, Merry Kick-mas
Chapter 7

STOCKINGS

Hang up the stockings tin man,
I need something to kick with,
because this holiday season
you're all in for a socking.
Fa-la-la-la-thwack!

'TWAS THE NIGHT

'Twas the night before Kick-mas,
when all through the dojo
not a bird was tweeting, not even a crow;
The sais were hung by the swords with care
in hopes that Santa Ninja would be there.

The children were kicked in the head,
with visions of punching bags kyai-ing in dread.
And sensei in their gi, and I in my sparring gear,
had just set up for a long night of fear.

When out on the mats there arose such a clatter,
I sprang from the side to fight the mad hatter.
Away to the back, I used my angles wise,
for the kickin-ing was no surprise.

The enemy ninjas on the eve of attack,
gave the luster of the belt made of black.
When, what to my wondering eyes should appear,
but a karate master, a jolly warrior was there.

With a little ol' hit, so lively and quick,
I knew in the moment I had seen the best kick.
For the enemy couldn't be the way they deprave,
for an elbow, and a punch, I knew the day was saved.

12 DAYS OF KICK-MAS
A CLASSIC CAROLING SONG BY JOSHUA CROCKER

On the first day of Kick-mas
my true love gave to me,
a puppy in a white gi.

On the second day of Kick-mas
my true love gave to me,
two shiny sais
and a puppy in a white gi.

On the third day of Kick-mas
my true love gave to me,
three savate kicks,
two shiny sais,
and a puppy in a white gi.

On the fourth day of Kick-mas
my true love gave to me,
four throwing stars,
three savate kicks,
two shiny sais,
and a puppy in a white gi.

On the fifth day of Kick-mas
my true love gave to me,
five sparring rings,
four throwing stars,
three savate kicks,
two shiny sais,
and a puppy in a white gi.

On the sixth day of Kick-mas
my true love gave to me,
six sticks a-smacking,
five sparring rings,
four throwing stars,
three savate kicks,
two shiny sais,
and a puppy in a white gi.

On the seventh day of Kick-mas
my true love gave to me,
seven blades a-slicing,
six sticks a-smacking,
five sparring rings,
four throwing stars,
three savate kicks,
two shiny sais,
and a puppy in a white gi.

On the eighth day of Kick-mas
my true love gave to me,
eight gloves a-punching,
seven blades a-slicing,
six sticks a-smacking,
five sparring rings,
four throwing stars,
three savate kicks,
two shiny sais,
and a puppy in a white gi.

On the ninth day of Kick-mas
my true love gave to me,
nine side kicks flying,
eight gloves a-punching,
seven blades a-slicing,
six sticks a-smacking,
five sparring rings,
four throwing stars,
three savate kicks,
two shiny sais,
and a puppy in a white gi.

On the tenth day of Kick-mas
my true love gave to me,
ten belts a-tying,
nine side kicks flying,
eight gloves a-punching,
seven blades a-slicing,
six sticks a-smacking,
five sparring rings,
four throwing stars,
three savate kicks,
two shiny sais,
and a puppy in a white gi.

On the eleventh day of Kick-mas
my true love gave to me,
eleven nunchucks chucking,
ten belts a-tying,
nine side kicks flying,
eight gloves a-punching,
seven blades a-slicing,
six sticks a-smacking,
five sparring rings,
four throwing stars,
three savate kicks,
two shiny sais,
and a puppy in a white gi.

203 -- A VERY, MERRY KICK-MAS

On the twelfth day of Kick-mas
my true love gave to me,
twelve pies a-soaring,
eleven nunchucks chucking,
ten belts a-tying,
nine side kicks flying,
eight gloves a-punching,
seven blades a-slicing,
six sticks a-smacking,
five sparring rings,
four throwing stars,
three savate kicks,
two shiny sais,
and a puppy in a white gi!

JINGLE

A punching bag is the gift to bash,
cause it's the gift that'll last and last.
So give the gift you know won't fail,
from Kicky-Punchy's adversary sale.

Most bags fall apart by Kick-mas,
but Punchy's is strong to the core.
Most everything is kicked around,
beatings you can't ignore.

At Oklahoma's strongest punchers,
we'll break a wood board too.
So give the gift you know won't fail,
from Kicky-Punchy's adversary sale.

ONWARD AND UP

Happy holidays everyone.
Onward and up and what not.
Sitting at the dinner table,
where has the time gone?
Wasn't it just January when I was a melodramatic fool?
The most magical place on earth,
the Niners won in the snow,
before they lost next week's show.
I sat on a bus with my earbuds in,
reminiscing the happy thoughts and the sad ones.
Wasn't it just June?
Summer heat, I found a new beat.
Out in the world, it's just me.
Wasn't it just October?
Pumpkin spice is now peppermint ice.
I'm an angsty poet, don't I know it.

Sitting at the dinner table,
where has the time gone?
Weren't we supposed to be kids forever?
But now it's college trips, dating,
bad words, growth spurts, and drinking.
Growing up is the name of the game.
And I'm not playing by the rules.
Onward and up, I guess.

Is this it?
How many more days like this do I get?
You all want to hear my dark secrets,
but I don't really have any.
Ha, I'm not a deviant like the rest of you,
I'm just the boring kid reading.
Well adult now, technically speaking.
I still do karate and watch cartoons,
I play games like tag and hide and seek.
Remember those times?
Onward and up, I guess.

Sitting at the dinner table,
where has the time gone?
I'm smiling, taking in every second I can.
But here's my secret if you must know:
I'm going to miss this, miss being a kid.
And I'm the oldest still, you all will follow after soon.
I'm fine with growing up,
but do you have to grow up too?
Does the band have to break up?
I can write another hit single, just wait.
I can sit here all I want, but time won't wait.
I'm not afraid of things changing,
or growing up, or new adventures.
Just when you go and do something awesome,
don't forget about the times we did karate together.
Onward and up.

CAROLING IN THE LIVING ROOM
A REMIX OF EXCERPTS FROM 'MY LAST CHRISTMAS'

Caroling in the living room at Grammy's house, every year we get excited for it. There's nothing like a sleigh ride with you. The kids host the show and it's the performance of the year. Every season it seems to be harder and harder to get prepared, I reckon. Imagine a string, pulling each and all of us in different directions. Will life steal what the holiday beckons?

We were kids and for some reason I thought those times would never end. I was too busy growing up to see you all doing the same. Do you feel as lost as me without each other?

Miss, I'm starting to realize I think more than I show. That's enough! If I keeping fretting about what I'll miss then I'd lose time to smile, and I rather smile at every snowflake falling then the ones melting.

SNOWY FIELD

A ninja in the snowy Rockies,
wearing a white suit instead of black;
a white belt on their new journey.
The cold eats at you,
the frost will fight you.
Amongst the avalanche signs
he creeps silently.
Facing a wild boar, he won't roar.
A ninja wearing a white suit,
faces challenges in the snowy fields.
On search for a new journey,
discovering what it means to learn.
Once upon a night,
a ninja reached his goal.
But now, once more, the snowy fields take hold.
Blights to fight, enemies in need of understanding.
A new start, a journey ahead.
But that's the truth.
When you climb the mountain,
you'll finally understand what it means,
now that you have to climb down.
A ninja in the snowy Rockies,
wearing a white suit instead of black,
a black belt starting their real journey.
For the journey starts at the summit.

211 -- A VERY, MERRY KICK-MAS

SANTA NINJA

Who's that a-tappin' on the roof top?
Tapity-tap-tap. Tapity-tap-tap.
Once a year the man with a red gi
and a white belt flies above the trees.
He visits our dojo late one night
to fight the gremlins and evil blight.
His spirit is filled with jolly, holly,
and by golly, vindictive tendencies.

Who's that a-tappin' on the roof top?
Tapity-tap-tap. Tapity-tap-tap.
He has his flying side kick to guide the way,
he moves with a gracious, dancing ballet.
Each lil' ninja boy and girl look toward the skies,
to see him deliver gifts of katanas and sais.
His spirit fills the air with a new toy, joy,
and oh boy, this Kick-mas morning
we'll know Santa Ninja made his way
to our dojo to celebrate and save the day.

"One of my favorite Kick-mas traditions is the Baking of the Twelve Pies. Each year martial artists bake twelve pies to enjoy and share with their training partners. A few martial artists will spend all day baking pies with one another before throwing a party to eat and celebrate together. It is custom to throw one of the pies at your instructor's face. It's all great fun and a way to bond with friends and family during the holiday season.

The customary pies are as follow: cherry, pecan, cinnamon apple, strawberry rhubarb, banana cream, mud/chocolate, blueberry, cranberry orange, pumpkin, sweet potato, lemon meringue, and macadamia coconut. This is the usual lineup of pies, but you are welcome to substitute pies for you and your friends! Some people only bake a few pies and some bake even more to be sure everyone at their dojo gets a slice or two and who knows, maybe a few leftovers to take home as well!"

PAIOSAMU KATA

Ho-ho-ho! It's the most festive kata, Paiosamu.
Lift up your hands and grab the star,
hold it against your heart. Rei and ready stance.

Slip to the left, get to the inside.
Chop down a tree for the festivities.
With a shuto strike from the side,
then shuto straight down and to the inside.
Grab the tree and toss it in the bed of the truck.
Turn to the right and chop down another tree.
Your strikes like a swift axe against lumber,
finish with a toss like a slingshot so they may slumber.

Take an evening out on the ice,
let your left foot glide behind you,
let your partner soar right by you.
Turn around and pick up your skates,
Twirl in the air like a winter butterfly.
Slice the ice with the blade of your right foot.
Take it back around the other way,
with your right foot gliding right by.
Dazzle and sparkle against the sheet of sleet.

Take an evening in the park with your love,
hold their hand close. Lift up a mug of cocoa.
Take a break from the daily grind.
Drop a candy cane into the mix if you're so inclined.

Turn to the left and pull out a match.
It's time to light the candles with an uppercut.
Ignite the first three, low, mid, to high.
Switch your feet, pull out a match on the right.
Ignite the next three, low, mid, to high.
Switch your feet, pull out a match on the left.
Ignite the last three, low, mid, and step the last time.

We have a pie to throw, so let's get to baking!
Turn around and step into the kitchen with me.
Carry a plate with the fruit on the right,
throw it in the mix with a left punch,
then slide up and slice it with an elbow strike.
Turn left, throw the pie at your instructor's face.
Spice things up with an extra punch,
make it a twist hit to the ribs and
hook back into the stomach region.

Grab the lights and string them up on the tree.
Turn behind you, and hang up five ornaments,
and finish with the star on the top of leaves.
A kick for each point of the star,
first a front kick, round kick on the left,
second a front kick, round kick on the right,
and to top it all off, a final side kick shining bright.

The night is almost here, Santa Ninja is near.
he will fly across the sky with his flying side kick,
and for all martial artists deliver Kick-mas cheer.

KICK-MAS MIRACLE
A SOMBER HOLIDAY SONG BY JOSHUA CROCKER

Light another candle, fry a latke.
Pray to baby Jesus, go out caroling.
The season is greeting us.
I want to feel the magic in the air,
but there's still fighting. Fighting over nothing.
It's cold out there. Are they freezing?
Presents and movies. Dreidels and wreaths.
What are we trying to distract ourselves from?
Are we really happy?
Or are we just done fighting?

It'll take a Kick-mas miracle for me.
To end the shouting, I say humbug.
It'll take more than gift-wrapped jewelry
to make us pretty again.
Let's go out and fight. That's right.
It'll take a Kick-mas miracle for me.
Let's laugh in the snow. Kick a snowman.
I'm done crying in the department store.
Let's pick up our feet and take to the street.
We'll make this holiday season ours again.

Happy holidays in a festive time of year,
celebrate every day. Fake the cheer.
Santa Ninja is on his way to save us.
Save us from our self-made prison cells.
There's music on the car radio,
that we'll cuss along to in winter traffic.
We've stopped reflecting. There's just anxiety.
What will it take to end the misery?
Where have the happy memories hid themself?
We'll just keep fighting,
families breaking at the dinner table.
Children screaming. Others are freezing.
Are we really happy?
Or are we just done fighting?

It'll take a Kick-mas miracle for me.
To end the shouting, I say humbug.
It'll take more than gift-wrapped jewelry
to make us pretty again.
Let's go out and fight. That's right.
It'll take a Kick-mas miracle for me.
Let's laugh in the snow. Kick a snowman.
I'm done crying in the department store.
Let's pick up our feet and take to the street.
We'll make this holiday season ours again.

There's a war on Kick-mas.
Zealots are taking away the happiness.
They hoard the love.
Capitalists are taking away the wonder.
They hoard the riches.
It's time for us to stand up.
Don't let our families break apart.
We can't let the cold freeze us up.
We'll simply have to fight.
Fight each other with love.
Stop the shouting. Quit the arguing.
And let's punch each other the right way.
That's what it's about.
Kick-mas is almost here.
Are we going to fight a war?
Or fight together for fun?
It's up to us to make the season ours again.

It'll take a Kick-mas miracle for me.
To end the shouting, I say humbug.
It'll take more than gift-wrapped jewelry
to make us pretty again.
Let's go out and fight. That's right.
It'll take a Kick-mas miracle for me.
Let's laugh in the snow. Kick a snowman.
I'm done crying in the department store.
Let's pick up our feet and take to the street.
We'll make this holiday season ours again.

There's self-defense and there's self-regret.
Put down the screen.
Don't let yourself scream.
And hold close your loved ones.
Hold close your partner,
and finish with a takedown.
Eat jelly donuts and gingerbread.
Give with your heart, fight with love.
It'll take a Kick-mas miracle.
It'll take a Kick-mas miracle.
End the shouting, let's start fighting.
Are we happy? Let's be happy.
Are we ready to fight all night?
Spar and punch one another.
No more division, no more shouting.
Just fighting for fun.
It'll take a Kick-mas miracle.
It'll take a Kick-mas miracle.
No more panic attacks at holiday parties.
We're the band of martial artists
who will punch and kick with a smile.
Hold hands, share our jackets, block and counter.
We'll make the kyais and happy songs seem louder.
Our fighting is more than 'over nothing.'
To start the joy, I say 'tis the season for us.
It'll take a Kick-mas miracle for me.

"Martial artists are a weird bunch. We fight our best friends. We punch each other. We kick each other. And yet, we all would do it again. There's too much anger out there. There's the fear of missing out that has led to a commercialism nightmare. There's the fear of disaster on the news. But just remember, there's more to Kick-mas then the fear. It's about the people we get to kick, the friends we've made. Let's fight the right way and quit the arguing.

Hi-ya! Merry Kick-mas to the lot of you!"

THAT HOLIDAY FEELING

You feel that?
The magic is back.
Don't let the world take it away.
Sales come and go.
Evil blights rise and die.
But tonight, it's just us.

You feel that?
The magic is back.
Let Santa Ninja take care of the danger.
We'll laugh and smile.
We'll give and feast.
For tonight, with love we fight. *And pie.*

BLUE BELT

Every punch he makes,
every kick you take,
Bob's fighting is pretty great.
The blue belt fighter has been practicing.
He's worked out his arms,
for a faster backfist, you can't back away.
A strong hook on the right,
packs a powerful punch from the left.
His legs as sturdy as an oak tree,
every stance in his katas are
perfectly still, like a maple tree.
Training makes perfect,
and even more training takes no complaining.
Bob knows he can keep growing,
that every second learning is worth the hard work.
As long as his arms keep punching,
as long as his legs keep kicking,
he'll be an unstoppable fighter to beat.

A MUSICAL EXTRAVAGANZA

Good tidings to you, and all of your kicks.
Good tidings for Kick-mas
and a happy coup de poing.
We wish you a merry Kick-mas.
We wish you a merry Kick-mas.
We wish you a merry Kick-mas
and a happy coup de poing.

****

It's beginning to look a lot like Kick-mas.
Tonfas make for décor.
But the prettiest sight to see is the black eye
that will be leaving your face so sore.

****

It's the most wonderful time of the year,
with the kids fighting and yelling,
and sensei is shouting, "Keep your hands up here!"

****

I'll be bruised for Kick-mas. Oh, it hurts so much.
Please have ice and Tylenol ready to help relieve me.

****

Jingle yell, jingle yell, your face I'll rock.

Silent night, let's start a fight.
Strike my palm, all with spite.

****

Kick-mas time is here,
bloodied my dear.
Fun for all, the children brawl,
strike your enemies with fear.

****

O come, all ye frightful, hateful and rambunctious.
O come ye, o come ye to the sparring ring.

****

It hit upon a midnight fear,
that goriest song of old.
From ninjas fighting near the snow
to punch through hearts of cold.

****

Deck you all with elbows and kalis,
fa-la-la-la, la-la-la-la!

****

Frederick, the red-nosed fighter
had a very bloody nose.
And if you ever saw it, you would say oh-no!

227 -- A VERY, MERRY KICK-MAS

Our finest hits we bring. Pa-rum-pum-pum-pum.
Our kicks will sting. Pa-rum-pum-pum-pum.
Shall I hit you. Pa-rum-pum-pum-pum.

****

I just want you for my own,
more than you could ever know.
Make my wish come true, baby,
all I want for Kick-mas is to hit you.

****

And since we have a face to throw,
kick your foe, kick your foe, kick your foe!

****

Rockin' around the Kick-mas tree,
at the Kick-mas party hop.
Punching bags hung where you can see,
every couple tries to pop.

****

We're practicing throws and falling,
and friends are cheering for you.
Come on, it's lovely weather,
for a fair fight together with you.
Come on, it's lovely weather,
for a fair fight together with you.

A WINTER LETTER

Dear you,

I can't wait for this Kick-mas day. Think of all the times we shared, all the times we cheered. It's getting colder out, but you make my heart warm. There's something about it, about the cold. It makes me feel alive.

I'm trying. Trying to become a better fighter. To protect myself and protect you. Trying to become a better teacher. To make a difference in the world. Trying to become a better friend. Because you deserve my best.

Whether Santa Ninja comes or not, we can sing merrily. We've made it all year. All of our fears, all of our troubles, for a moment we can forget. Because we made it this far. And together, I don't think anything can stop us.

There's more to self-defense than kicking. If this Kick-mas season has taught me anything, it's that. There's love in the air. We love training in karate, tae kwon do, and whatever it may be. I love kicking you in the face. And I love it when you kick me back. Isn't what that's what this season is all about?

Keep fighting. Keep your guard up. Keep your spirits up. Don't be afraid to cry, because you'll stand back up again. We're tougher than we believe we are. As we approach the new year, smile. We get do it all over again.

I can't help but let my imagination get the best of me. It's the lights, the snow, the crisp air. Hot coffee and a warm fireplace. The kicks on the bag. I'll write a love story, I'll make a scrapbook, I'll sing a song.

All the memories, I want to remember them all. The good ones and bad ones. I'll remember the challenges I overcame, the laughter on the mats, the time spent together. I'll remember the losses, the blood and bruises, the frustration. Most of all I'll remember the twinkle in your eyes when you threw me to the ground with glee.

There's so much more I want to write to you that I just can't put it all into words. We'll be back on the mats soon enough. Enjoy a couple days off. Best wishes to you and your family. Keep kicking!

With love,
Joshua

The Cooler Karate Kid
Chapter 8

"I'm Joshua Crocker, lyrical genius.
The cooler karate kid."

THIRTEEN AND COUNTING

The first move I learned was probably a front kick,
honestly I don't remember anymore.
I used to train in tae kwon do and got
annoyed when people said I did karate.
Now I do both and don't care.
They're both the same anyway,
they just use different words
to describe the same thing.
I remember practicing board breaks at home.
I would memorize katas with my parents.
During class I would always play games in my mind.
I still do. Focusing is hard. What was I saying?
I liked playing chess as a kid.
And making train tracks around the house.
My sister and I trained together;
we practiced by punching each other.
I'm pretty sure she started it.
I used to lack confidence.
I was a smart kid,
but there's always someone smarter.
Apparently martial arts helps you build confidence.
I guess karate or whatever is supposed to stop you
from getting hurt, learn to stand up for yourself.
So, that's why my parents made me start.
Did it work? Eh, I'll let you decide on that one.

WHAT DO YOU WANT TO BE

What do you want to be when you grow up?
When I was pretty young I said I would be a
librarian, firefighter, or ninja when I was older.
Well...
Now I'm a reading-adverse, pyrophobic black belt.
I write books, put out fires, and teach karate.
I hope five-year-old me is proud.

SOCCER AND FOOTBALL

Soccer, I hardly know her.
Football, that's exactly where my foot's going.
Americans and Europeans
fighting over the naming rights.
Well one of you kicks towards the goal,
the other kicks when they give up.
When I kick you'll both know what's up
They each need eleven folks running around,
all I need is one kick to the head to win.
So who's the real winner here?
Canadian Football will have you down a play sooner,
I'll take you down with a sweep to the leg.
Fake the play, in a fake made-up game.
Take a dive if someone grazes your shin.
Because if you get hurt, cry to the refs.
While you do that, I'll get punched in the ribs.
And I won't even bat an eye.
Play well on defense, I'll stay with self-defense.
Here's the kicker,
while you both bicker,
I'll just snicker,
cause in the end I'm the best kicker.

WILL YOU FOCUS!

"Hey goobers, stop talking and just do the move!"
I shout at a couple knucklehead students talking.
I get it, chatting with friends is fun,
but now is the time to focus and train.
I walk away to keep assisting students.

Fading, rippling, other various flashback effects.
"What do you think they'll do with the character in
the next movie? It was such a good cliffhanger..."
I keep rambling to my friend about the Avengers
movies, the new Zelda game, and probably Lego.
Ha, nerd.
"Will you focus!" my instructor shouts to us.
I sigh and we keep drilling blocks with a bo staff.
We keep practicing, but my mind still wanders.
Fading, rippling, other various flashback effects.

I turn back to watch the students I just talked to.
They're already chatting again. I sigh.
These kids are always talking about something,
sports and school, making cleverly dumb jokes,
middle-school-level flirting, or just being goofballs.
They are kids after all.
As long as they're learning, let them have fun.
Also, I was such a nerd.

STICKER LINE

I was an excited kid.
Chatting with my new friends,
waiting in line to get a sticker.
I can't wait for the next game day.

I was an awkward preteen.
Handing out stickers for the wall,
looking over at you with a dumb joke,
my secret plan to hear your laugh.

I was a calm teacher.
Looking over my student's shoulder,
teaching them what to do,
watching them help after class.

BULLY DEFENSE

Hey kids! Let's learn some bully defense!
First, if they grab you, just move your arm like so.
Awesome! If they try to punch you, just slip.
Great! Now if they keep picking on you,
just go let an adult, like a teacher or parent know.
If they call you names, don't get mad,
just say, "Thank you!" and move on.
Remember to always be nice to others.
Alright, that's all for now, go team!

...

Are they gone?
Good. I don't want to break their spirits.
Because in real life the bullies never go away.
The reality is bullies will push you to the ground
and when you stand up they'll spit in your face.
They'll make your life a living hell if you let them.
To them, if your different then you're useless.
As I look back at my time growing up it
just seems like the world wants you to fail.
If you make one mistake, they'll eat you alive.
The bullies, the people in charge, the cliques,
none of them want you to succeed.
Being a kid, is, um, it's tough. Not gonna lie.
Those kids need their optimism,
because without it, pfft. I don't envy them.

GROWING UP IS HARD
A KID'S POP-PUNK SONG BY JOSHUA CROCKER

Growing up is hard, it's tough being a kid,
for some reason the adults don't like us.
My name is Davie, I've got more homework
than I've got time in the day to play.
I have to write an essay on Lord of the Flies,
and the author, some old dude by the way,
thinks that if kids were left in charge
we would delve into a chaotic, violent fray.
I don't know, it seems like the adults
already got that one down.

I'm so confused,
you keep telling me to put down my electronics,
but what am I going to do instead?
All the books in the library are banned now.
Pfft. I'm bored. It's getting too hot to play outside.
Video games cause violence,
board games are demonic,
and TV rots your brain.
It kinda sounds like you're just making stuff up.

Growing up is hard, it's tough being a kid,
for some reason the adults don't like us.
I don't know why, I'm just a kid,
what did I do wrong?
If my generation is spoiled,
why are school lunches so expensive?
Growing up is hard,
books are out of style, bullies are everywhere,
stranger danger, racist county rangers,
and they just installed metal detectors at school.

I'm so confused,
one of my friends isn't allowed to wear a dress,
but another said her school forces her to.
My favorite teacher was fired for the
cool new flags she hung up in her room.
Pfft. Being a kid is the worst.
On the first day of school we had to list our
favorite things and draw pictures of our family,
but Timmy said he had to leave his picture blank
because he isn't allowed to talk about his parents.
That doesn't seem fair,
I wish I could get out of schoolwork.

Growing up is hard, it's tough being a kid,
for some reason the adults don't like us.
I don't know why, I'm just a kid,
what did I do wrong?
If my generation is spoiled,
why are school lunches so expensive?
Growing up is hard,
books are out of style, bullies are everywhere,
stranger danger, racist county rangers,
and they just installed metal detectors at school.

I'm so confused,
why is it so dangerous to be a kid?
The adults all say they're looking out for us,
but every month another school is on the news
because some kids were killed. Uhh...
I'm not going to lie, I'm kinda getting a little scared.
Now I don't really understand all that
boring government stuff, but shouldn't we fix that?
Pfft. Maybe they're only allowed to make up
so many new rules every month?
I'm still confused then why this month they chose to
stop letting that one lady read to us at the library
and instead kept the rules letting kids get married.
I'm never going to get married; girls are gross
and I heard boys go to Jupiter to get more stupider.
We have a real cootie crisis on our hands
and no one is even talking about it!

Growing up is hard, it's tough being a kid,
for some reason the adults don't like us.
I don't know why, I'm just a kid,
what did I do wrong?
If my generation is spoiled,
why are school lunches so expensive?
Growing up is hard,
books are out of style, bullies are everywhere,
stranger danger, racist county rangers,
and they just installed metal detectors at school.

I'm so confused,
why is everything such a mess?
I thought all those adults were pretty smart,
after all they've already gone to school and college.
They get to drive their cars
and watch all the cool action movies,
but I'm just stuck with this bully
who told me my hair looks ugly.
I share food with my friend Jane,
because she can't eat lunch anymore;
her parents can't afford it.
Kidnappings and shootings are on the rise.
Bullies hate me, cyberbullies say I should die,
and even the government people are bullying us now.
Pfft. Growing up is hard.

Hey psst, kids, I'm going to write the next part
in Comic Sans so the adults can't read it.

It's okay to be different.
It's okay to have friends who are different,
and you're the one who gets a chance
to treat them amazing, regardless.

Also remember, reading is fun!
And hey, if you're like me and don't like to sit down
and read because your brain races across the place,
then try an audiobook!
Also, thanks for reading my book.
Writing is really fun too; you should give it a try.

Here is a list of a few great books
that old people have tried to ban before.
Be sure to check them out from
the library next time you're there:

"And Tango Makes Three", "Are You There God? It's Me,
Margaret", "Bridge to Terabithia", "Charlotte's Web",
"Diary of a Young Girl", "Drama," "The Hate U Give", "I
Am Jazz", "The Lion, the Witch, and the Wardrobe",
"Melissa (formerly George)", "Of Mice and Men",
"Something Happened in our Town", "Stamped (For Kids):
Racism, Antiracism, and You", "To Kill a Mockingbird",
"Where the Sidewalk Ends", "A Wrinkle in Time"

"I hope one day I'm popular enough of a writer that some 'concerned parent' tries to get my books banned from schools or libraries."

YOU'VE GOT THIS

Even if things seem tough, just remember,
life is a journey.
You'll have your ups and downs,
your wins and losses,
but you can do this. You've got this.

Even if that bag seems too heavy now,
you'll knock it over eventually.
Even if that kick is too challenging,
you'll figure it out with some help.
Even if the bullies knock you down,
you'll just have to stand up again.
Even if earning your black belt seems impossible,
you'll get there. It takes time, just stick with it.

Things may seem tough, but you're tougher.
You've got this.

"Every generation has had television and movies that influenced kids to start martial arts. Karate Kid, Teenage Mutant Ninja Turtles, Power Rangers. Nowadays, Cobra Kai is the hit show that everyone watches. We get a quite a few kids who come in to try class, and the reason they want to learn martial arts is because they watched Cobra Kai. A show with violence, cussing, rivalries. The show has students getting into fights with no gear, people beat up and bloodied, intense decade-long grudges. And as a martial arts teacher who teaches many young kids – I myself started when I was six years old – have to say in reality this show is... absolutely spot on."

YEAH, I'D SAY I'M PRETTY TOUGH

For years I had never broken a bone.
Well guess what, I was at the dojo
the other day and broke my toe.
No biggie, I walked it off and hopped back on
the mats to teach classes the rest of the night.
I'm just that tough.
How did I break my toe?
Oh, well... I stubbed my pinky toe on a door
during the five-year-old's class.
But to be fair that door has been
attending our dojo for eight years,
so it's practically a karate master by now!

249 -- THE COOLER KARATE KID

CHILD PRODIGY

Karate master, epic fighter.
An innate talent for being awesome.
Can get up in front of a class
and charm them in an instant.
The child prodigy.
A fantastic martial artist, will kick you in the head,
every time they elbow you it will leave a bruise.
Not to mention their creativity, an artist of life,
well-spoken, smart, a sparkling leader. (Humble too)
It's easy to be this competitive when
it's in your nature to just keep winning.
The child prodigy.
Every joke they tell is hilarious at once,
will be your friend after five minutes.
Crisp katas, the fierce look of a fighter,
always has a list in their head,
a list of ways they can beat you.
The child prodigy.
Karate master, epic fighter.
A fantastic martial artist; will punch you in the nose.
Every kyai pierces the air, a natural singer,
every song lyric lingers in the hearts of all.
Get ready to be wowed, charmed, and amazed,
by the child prodigy... my sister.

BUNKBED BUNKAI

Throw a pillow, I'll block with a book.
Make a blanket fort with troops for support.
Stuffed animals by the front gate.
Lt. Peter and Sgt. Tigey on each side.
Toss a miniature football like a grenade,
fight with a Lego sword, parry the enemy.
Jump from the top bunk, land with a thunk.
Add a punch, elbow, and knee.
Scrape and claw, retreat to the comforter cavern.
Plan an ambush at the quilt quarry.
One last attack with a flying (*falling*) side kick,
watch out for the spinning of foam nunchucks.
And the best part,
in the end we can go eat ice cream!

253 -- THE COOLER KARATE KID

VIRTUAL LEARNING

I hated virtual learning.
Trying to train without a partner.
At home it was always cramped,
at the dojo teaching was exhausting.
Talking to a camera is nowhere near
the same as seeing everyone's face.

But the one good thing
was the chance to do something,
anything really, something I love.
So sure, it was tiring and different,
but it was the little time each day
I got to see another person for a bit
and just train for fun.

NOSTALGIA IS IN THE JOURNEY
A REFLECTIVE ACOUSTIC FOLK SONG BY JOSHUA CROCKER

So, um, before I earned my junior black belt I had to make this project about my martial arts' journey. It was a martial arts version of this card game I liked. The game is in a box that is currently sitting in the back room at the dojo. Being the creative perfectionist I am, I always wonder if I could have done a better job with my project. To be fair, I was twelve. Anyway, here's a song about martial arts.

A bo staff clashing against another,
rainy skies giving way for sunny days.
Watching the Karate Kid for the first time,
the last episode of my favorite show on the mats.
Zoom classes, Chung Ji in the backyard's right side,
brochures on door frames, now just a picture frame.
Learning self-defense on Tower Drive,
a sunset behind the water tower and train tracks.
With every second gone by, and every sweat drop,
every teardrop, it's everything that made me.
Oh, you see where I've come from. I fought for what I
got, and learned the journey is where the heart is at.

A math joke made you laugh, algebra on the
white board, and each knee in Japanese.
Masks and hand sanitizer, an excuse or two,
rosewater, and ice cream stains on a white gi.
Water balloon fights and the reject in river nights.
Camp games, capture the flag, and pineapple pizza.
Forms and more, learn new katas, and learn some more.
Flags on the wall; red, white, a little blue.
Dodgeball, a pool noodle, an old man, nukes falling.
Talking in the back, secrets and feelings, cleaning too.
Oh, you see where I've come from. I fought for I got,
and learned the journey is where the heart is at.

Ornaments and cocoa, Kick-mas morning,
pies for no reason, constant storming.
Ice days and classes with my stuffed friends,
video games and word puzzles with my real friends.
A holiday greeting led to a meeting; I need a drink.
Santa Ninja bringing gifts, costume parties,
a yearbook with pictures of faces and mask coverings.
From neighbors, game nights, now snow training.
A weapons class in the park, my liberal use of snark,
come the winter nights sparring fights in the dark.
Oh, you see where I've come from. I fought for what I
got, and learned the journey is where the heart is at.

Holding tae kwon do stances, kicking and slipping,
lying flat on my back and laughing at it.
The chatter of little kids and their trains,
all the while I'm trying to train.
A pancake breakfast before tournaments.
Three trophies and second place, I won only once.
Black belt testings, a future arsonist lighting a fire.
Bloody noses, losing fights, that damn bag at midnight.
An old mall, a white stripe, the park one last time,
and starting it all over again.
Oh, you see where I've come from. I fought for what I
got, and learned the journey is where the heart is at.

Oh, you see where I've come from. I fought for what I
got, and learned the journey is where the heart is at.

STILL DOING KARATE

My friends all quit eventually.
We trained together for years.
I don't remember a lot of the specifics
of what I learned as a kid on these mats,
but I do remember the other people there.
Some of them made it pretty far.
Purple belt, brown belt, even black belt.
I hope they all will do great elsewhere.
High school, college, and so on.
I'm still the kid who does karate.
Sometimes I run into one of those adults
who've known me since I was a baby.
They ask me if I still do tae kwon do.
I tell them yeah, I'm actually a teacher now.
This is my job.
I'm still on these mats.
I remember when my friends left,
I had no one to train with. I made new friends.
Some of them left too. Then I found more friends.
I'll teach a new generation of karate kids,
I'll make more friends,
and I'll keep training on these mats.
And that's just my story.
I'm the kid who does karate.

"I'm not that old. I finished high school within the last couple years. But I've recently realized there are students I teach who weren't even born when I earned my black belt. We have kids younger than our dojo who just passed their orange belt test. Our most recent students who tested for their junior black belts were both 1 year old when I started training in tae kwon do years ago. So I'm still not that old, but sheesh, everyone else just keeps getting younger."

A LONG AND CONVOLUTED STORY

So this next poem is sort of a long and convoluted story about people, mostly people I know. Also people I don't know, well not anymore anyway. But it could also be about you. Any story could be about you really, because well, you're the one reading the story, right? A story with no reader is just forgotten words.

So it was summer. One of my top four favorite seasons. I was going about normal business, teaching classes, training, ectara. I actually think this day was one of the first classes I taught. I don't remember specifically, but it was around this time I taught a beginner's class and I just remember thinking I nailed it. I mean, by no means was I perfect, but that was the class that gave me the confidence I could be a good teacher.

Well I had this plan, you see. To get a picture, with me in it. And I guess other people too, but I was the most important person in that picture. Then I was going to send that picture to someone to make fun of them for not being in said picture. I never said it was a good plan. Well, they ruined my plan, because they ended up sneaking their way into my picture. Which to be clear, I was not expecting. All that make sense?

Anyway, I was in a good mood. Maybe it was from that class I taught, maybe it was because of a friend. See, I love to write. I love to talk and teach. I love to be alone with my brilliant thoughts and plans. But more than any of that I love having people in my life who mean something. Because people, that's what makes our lives special. The story of your life would be boring without anyone else. And the neat thing, a person you'll never know can be so important to someone else's story. I mean, just think about how important you may be to someone else's story.

Well as happy and obnoxious as I was, I was also still at work. Of course, kicking people is always a great part of working. I had this new student to work with that night. And see this is where stories can be so interesting, a person I didn't know, how they became a part of this long and convoluted story. Well I heard another instructor talking to her, giving me an insight to who she was. Her age, occupation, and by her shirt I could draw conclusions about how talented of a kicker she would be one day.

So as I'm working with this student, my mind was elsewhere. I'm thinking about this other person. You see, my first plan was ruined. Remember, the picture plan. So I came up with a second plan. Now this plan was a lot simpler, I was just going to talk to the person. I know, how crazy and brave I was.

I spent class preparing my second plan, which consisted of approximately two sentences. And after class I enacted my plan. It worked perfectly. So this is the part of the story I've written about before, blah-blah, ice cream, blah-blah, that dumb look on your face, blah-blah, sitting in a parking lot, blah-blah, no one cares. But apparently at the time I did. It wasn't an interesting story, but it was a story with people in it. And that's what I was interested in, people. Specific people who meant something to me and my story. But the part I hadn't realized was how the rest of the story would go. Because, well, here's the part I would only realize a couple years later.

People change. People leave. Sometimes people come back. New people get to meet you. But in every memory is a person, a person with their own story and life, but in that moment a person who was a part of your story. Now you may be thinking, "Joshua are you done rambling yet?" And well, no, not all.

People leave. Actually, that's what made that night so important to begin with. I've been skipping over the part of this story that started everything. This specific story isn't even mine. No, this is the story of someone else; I just hijacked it to have my own side story at the same time. People leave, important people, people who can bring others together. But that's what makes these moments so special.

What impact does that have? As I sit here telling this story to you now, I realize the people I'm writing to has changed. For better or worse, people change. A person that meant so much to so many, scratch that, a person who meant something to me left. And even if I hadn't realized it yet, it would change my story.

I said talking to a friend left me in a good mood. And on my drive home I was still in a good mood. But people change, and so would I. It wouldn't be long until I would take the memory of that night and blot it out of my mind. Because, for a moment there was this other person who was a part of my story, and I didn't realize that moment would change with time. Because later on, my next plan didn't work. And the one after that didn't either. And eventually, I lost. I got punched in the head and stomped off because of it. Not because I lost, but because of who I lost to and how I handled it. As people change, they fall out of touch, people are lost, and now a moment is just a memory.

Now I've lost two people. But little did I know at the time, maybe I had found another one. There's more to the story than memories. Because the person I met that night is now the person reading this long, rambling dialogue. Someone I barely knew became a part of the next chapter in my story. And I was right, she would become a talented kicker one day.

This story is about the first chorus I wrote, it was a song about the night I now see as the night I lost one person; but the first person to read that chorus was someone I just met. And as I was meeting this person, I was coming up with another one of my plans. I was crafting words in my head, while fate was crafting a story.

People come back. After they leave, people can still make a difference. Because we're all in different chapters of our own stories. And important people will remain important. People who helped make you who you are.

So now a couple years later I realize what that night meant: It meant nothing and everything. It was an intersection of time and with time, moments become memories and stories get new meanings. Sometimes 'goodbye' is just 'see you later,' and sometimes 'I hope you have a good night' is 'I hope you have a good life,' and sometimes 'It was nice getting to meet you' is 'I'm glad to have you as a friend.'

This is a story of people. There are people in all of our stories that forever will have their place there. And you, there will be someone who will forever remember you as a part of their story. Make sure that the part you play will always be a good one.

STAND UP

Why do the bullies keep picking on me?
I did what you told me to... I stood up for myself.
They pushed me to the floor and I stood up.
Then they just hit me again.
Why can't I just stop getting bullied?!
I'm supposed to be a martial artist.
They should be scared of me.
So, why does every strike I throw seem meaningless?
Why do the bullies keep hitting me?

Probably because you kept standing up.

"When you fall down you have two choices: you stay on the ground or you stand up. Admit defeat or fight back. And if you fight back, you might get knocked down again. Then you have to make the same choice again. You'll have to make the choice to stand up over and over again. But in the end if you do, you'll know nothing can keep you down. Keep standing up for yourself; keep standing up for the world.
The choice is yours. Lie down or stand up and fight."

BROWN BELT

Things have gotten intense.
A brown belt now, Bob is the best.
He's watched his friends fight in this war,
every kick makes another one sick.
He has always wanted to be a great fighter,
But in a time of necessity he kept training.
Every push-up made him stronger,
to the core every sit-up strengthens his might.
He is ready to put up a fight.
The war for the dojo has left him battle-scarred,
the look on his face is a calm stare,
the stare of a martial artist.
He faces up against his ultimate enemy.
This will be his greatest fight yet.
He must win, not for himself,
but for the people he has come to love.
So they fight! Bob had spent years learning,
he just wanted to train, get better one day at a time.
His footwork was unparalleled,
when knocked to the floor, he stood up again.
His posture incredible, every kick stung,
every strike was unforgettable, every kyai rung.
He stood stout like a tree trunk, swift as its leaves.
His team cheered him on from the side,
and in the end, battered and bruised, Bob won.

FIGHTING, FIGHTING: SAME, SAME

Hey, you ever get into fights when you were a kid?
Huh, plenty.
Yeah, but it wasn't like the problem I have, right?
Why? Fighting, fighting. Same, same.
Yeah, but you knew karate.
Someone always know more.

I was a kid when I learned how to punch.
I was short when I got kicked in the gut.
It hurt. Knocked the breath out of me.
I swore that I would never spar again.
Why bother if there is always someone bigger than me.
Always someone better than me.

You mean there were times
when you were scared to fight?
Always scare. Miyagi hate fighting.
Yeah, but you like karate.
So?

When I stood up I was mad.
I was mad I let myself get hurt.
Karate was supposed to help me stop getting hurt.
What's the point of self-defense if I keep getting hurt!
I love to train, I love to kick, so why am I no good?

So, karate's fighting. You train to fight.
That what you think?
No.
Then why train?

What's the point of self-defense?
I'm no martial artist, just some loser.
"Stand up. Walk it off," someone says.
Whatever. What has 'walking it off' ever done.
"Hey, sometimes we get hurt."
"Next time keep your hands up."

So I won't have to fight.
Miyagi have hope for you.

Fine. I put my helmet back on. I got hit again.
It hurt less this time, but I still don't understand
why I can't just block the hit entirely.
When I finally had enough, I hit them back.
I hit them as hard as I could, which with my scrawny
ten-year-old arms felt like a cat playfully pawing.
I'll just keep training until I can win every fight.
Until I can stop any hit from hurting me again.
And I did. And along the way I've been hit plenty.
I still get hit plenty. I hit back plenty too.
I kept training for my next fight.
And now, I've taken enough hits,
I finally don't feel the need to fight,
because I know no hit will be enough to stop me.

273 -- THE COOLER KARATE KID

I'M THE COOLER KARATE KID

Eat it Ralph Macchio, I'm the cooler karate kid.
The kid on the mats, the kid punching the bag.
I'm not here to brag, I'll raise the flag,
I'll kick you in the head twenty times.
Don't knock it down, I hold my leg, I'll never drown.
So smile now, this ain't the time to frown.

Oh! Charyut! Kick 'em kid. Say hey, rei, face off.
Kick 'em kid. Kick 'em in the head. Oh! Watch this!

I can get up quicker than you can take me down,
I'm the one running around, take the race downtown,
I'm faster, I'm stronger, in the ring I'm a monster.
But just you wait, I'm the kid you can't tag, let's go,
I'll fight in drag and still you won't take my swag.

Oh! Charyut! Kick 'em kid. Say hey, rei, face off.
Kick 'em kid. Kick 'em in the head. Oh! Watch this!

Crane kick!
You'll never see me put my hands to the side,
I win my fights on the first try Danny.
Now you can't deny, I'm ready for the moment,
push-ups, core exercise, I've built my thighs,
now my kicks make gravity defy.

Oh! Charyut! Kick 'em kid. Say hey, rei, face off.
Kick 'em kid. Kick 'em in the head. Oh! Watch this!

The kid jumping and leaping, the kid winning,
I've been on the mats since the beginning
and I'm still winning. Sweep the leg!
I play dirty, fight unfair, pull your hair,
winner's don't lose and I've already lost plenty.

Oh! Charyut! Kick 'em kid. Say hey, rei, face off.
Kick 'em kid. Kick 'em in the head. Oh! Watch this!

Wax on! Wax off!
I'm standing pretty, it's a gold medal kata show.
I may be petty. Regards, my fist says hello.
Life's unfair, so I'm always aware. Say a prayer,
I'm kicking your way, my legs on display,
I'm no karate nerd cliché, a fighter on a whim.
No, I'm a fighter out and in, the cooler karate kid.

Oh! Charyut! Kick 'em kid. Say hey, rei, face off.
Kick 'em kid. Kick 'em in the head. Oh! Watch this!

Wearing a black gi,
I'm the cooler karate kid.
That's me.

Self-Defense Class

Chapter 9

"Self-defense is taking the punch.
Ready to fight back, ready to stand up.
Let's keep singing, stayin' alive.
Keep reading, smilin' all the time.
These are songs about self-defense,
they're songs for you. Let's keep fighting."

MENTAL HEALTH, SELF-DEFENSE

You can learn karate, and you can learn jiu-jitsu,
but don't forget to learn to protect yourself
where you can't forget yourself.
Don't stay safe on the outside,
just to die on the inside,
because it's the one fight
you can't fight with your fists,
the fight we all need help to win.

You can learn knife and gun defense,
but when you're the one holding the blade,
it's your finger on the trigger, what does it matter?
Who's there to keep you safe if you feel alone?
Ask for a hug from someone who cares.
Being close to another won't always lead to a takedown,
you still need a solid base to not end on the ground.

You can learn karate, and you can learn jiu-jitsu,
and you can learn to keep your guard up,
they're always telling us to keep our guard up.
The truth is, at some point
you have to let your guard down.
You have to take a hit and cry,
and trust that you know how to get up again.

WHAT SHE WAS TOLD
A HEARTFELT ROCK SONG BY JOSHUA CROCKER

And she said she never learned,
she said she never cared about herself,
was taught to put others first,
and herself last.
It's what we heard as kids,
and it stuck with us
like a virus in our conscience.
Love others and stop loving yourself.

What she was told,
I heard it growing up too,
is to be kind, to be loving,
to smile every day for
the sake of everyone else.
What she was told,
the only way to be happy
is to be sure everyone else is happy.
What she was told,
looking out for yourself is selfish.
That the world would be a better place
if we only could only set aside our pride,
and yet now we don't know how to love ourselves.

We live in a world of priority,
where we have everything and nothing at once.
There's so much good left to do,
and so much love breathing in the air.
But our priorities are undefined. She was taught to
put God first, followed by her family, next her friends.
Care for the orphans, look out for the widows,
none of that's wrong. Love others, heal the world.
But how far does she have to drop in priority,
how long before she can tend to herself?
Because when you give everything,
you're left with nothing. Don't you see?
And if love dissipates, she'll suffocate.
My dear, it's okay to love yourself.

What she was told,
I heard it growing up too,
is to be kind, to be loving,
to smile every day for
the sake of everyone else.
What she was told,
the only way to be happy
is to be sure everyone else is happy.
What she was told,
looking out for yourself is selfish.
That the world would be a better place
if we only could only set aside our pride,
and yet now we don't know how to love ourselves.

They painted us a picture of a true family,
one where the wife spends every moment
loving her husband and caring for her kids.
Always there for them, no matter their pain.
But who is there for her,
when she hides from the world,
hoping no one sees her tears.
This feeling isn't absent, just out of sight.
We hide love so deep inside, only showing it
for those we care for; we keep them warm.
But she looks down, her shaking hands are so cold.
Every second caring for another,
never knowing how to care for herself.
My dear, it's okay to love yourself.

What she was told,
I heard it growing up too,
is to be kind, to be loving,
to smile every day for
the sake of everyone else.
What she was told,
the only way to be happy
is to be sure everyone else is happy.
What she was told,
looking out for yourself is selfish.
That the world would be a better place
if we only could only set aside our pride,
and yet now we don't know how to love ourselves.

So, she stopped caring.
Let herself drift way, like dust in the wind.
These tears won't go away,
they're a part of who we are,
what we grew up thinking was the only way.
Every day I try so desperately to get others
to think I'm great. I ask, "Do you like me?"
If I can just get another to smile, then I won't
have to deal with the fact I hate my own.
These tears are just who we are.
My dear, it's okay to love yourself.

Don't you see?
See the heartbreak living in her eyes?
Is there not enough time in the day
to help others and still let myself grow up?
And if anyone else feels this way,
you read these words, hear this song,
just know heartbreak isn't the only way.
Don't you see?
See the heartbreak living in her eyes?
She's trying so hard.
You can't save the world,
if you can't save yourself.
You can't fill the world with love,
if you can't find love in yourself.

What she was told,
I heard it growing up too,
is to be kind, to be loving,
I love you; will you love me too?
Please, I feel alone. I just don't know.
What she was told,
the only way to be happy
is to be sure everyone else is happy.
So why isn't she happy?
Why aren't we happy? Am I being selfish?
Would the world be a better place
if I only could set aside this pride?
Why don't we know how to love ourselves?
What she was told
stuck like a virus in our conscience.
Love others and stop loving yourself.

My dear, it's okay to love yourself.
My dear, it's okay.
It's okay. You'll be okay.
My dear, it's okay to love yourself.
It's okay, it's okay.
It's okay, my dear it's okay.
My dear, no matter what you were told,
it's okay to love yourself.

BUBBLE

I'm so sorry about that bloody nose I gave you.
I know you didn't ask for my fist
to, well, forcefully punch your face.
But then again,
you never asked permission to grab my arm,
despite the fact I don't know you.
Again, I'm so sorry I made you cry like a little baby.
But if I'm being honest, it was a little funny.
After all, I was just trying to mind my own business,
and you getting up in my bubble
was a little troubling to say the least.
To be fair, I didn't think I could punch that hard,
but watching you stumble back and trip over the
pantleg of your designer jeans would say otherwise.
And I'm also so sorry that no one believed you
when you tried backtracking by saying
you thought I was someone else.
It was just hard to believe because
as you grabbed my arm you did happen to say,
"Hey baby, I know I don't know you,
but I think you look-"
I am curious what you were going to say next,
but it was around that time my fist hit your face.
You know what, on second thought I'm not that sorry.

WARNING: DON'T TOUCH

Have you ever seen one of those
"Warning: Don't Touch" signs?
Maybe on the glass of a nuclear reactor,
the bars to the gorilla cage at the zoo,
or the dumpster out behind Taco Bell.
Well now let's pretend people have giant
floating "Warning: Don't Touch" signs too.
Because you really shouldn't just go around
touching people who don't want you to touch them.
It's a novel idea, I know.
Also have you ever heard of *disease*?
It's the thing that makes your nose sneeze.
Germs. Snot. Dirt. People are gross.
Which to circle back to my first point,
is another reason you should
keep your hands to yourself.
Capiche?

VALIDITY

Okay, one last thing. I'm being serious now.
Kid, you don't need a reason to be uncomfortable.
If you're uncomfortable that's reason enough.
That gut feeling is valid. You're valid.
If something feels wrong, speak up.
If you don't like the way someone is treating you,
whether they're breaking your personal space
or speaking like a jerk, then make them stop.
Let someone who cares for you know,
or just punch the moron if you have to.
If someone tries to invalidate your feelings, they tell
you you're 'overreacting' or being 'emotional,'
then go ahead and tune out their manipulative lies.
No one gets to tell you how you feel.
How would they even know?
The way you feel is valid.
You're valid.

"Every story needs an ending. But for better or worse, in real life things tend to be anti-climactic."

BLACK BELT

Standing over his defeated adversary,
a symbol of every challenge he has overcome.
Bob had become the hero we needed.
He had earned his black belt, the end of his final test.
A triumph among many, Bob truly was the best.
The war was not yet over, though.
And the story of Bob has one more chapter.
Just know, this is no victory, just tragedy.
Bob had become stern; he was tired of the fighting.
Worried for the sake of his family around.
His heart ached; his body was weary.
The other black belts became worried,
they knew Bob was the best fighter around,
their own teammate had become dangerous.
So they hatched a plan. They fought Bob as a team.
His punches hurt, so they chopped each arm off.
The speed of his kicks were fast, so off with his legs.
Just a torso now, the great fighter Bob was shocked.
His own friends, the family he loved,
they turned on him.
He had become too dangerous in their eyes.
The final part of the plan was to turn him to rubber.
They used their machine to immobilize him.
There he stood, Bob the once great fighter,
was now a punching bag.

What is the moral of the story?
Bob took every day to learn,
but now others use him to learn.
He trained to be a great fighter,
but in the end it wasn't enough to stay safe.
He protected his friends,
but they betrayed him.
This is the story of Bob the punching bag.
A tragic telling of a fall from glory.
There is no moral to this story.
Sometimes things just happen.

Sometimes the hero gets turned to rubber,
just sitting there limbless with a fighter's glare,
for others to train with, to kick and punch forever.

This is the story of a guy named Bob.

SONGS ABOUT SELF-DEFENSE -- 294

LOSE, LOSE

Some games make losers.
The game of life is alike.
It's a lose, lose scenario.
And that's just how it works.
You're a great fighter?
Well I hope you stay safe.
You're a good person?
Well I hope life goes your way.
But sometimes it's just lose, lose.
And we just have to deal with it,
accept it and hope we can move on.
Hope we can stay alive to
win again some other day.
Because no matter how hard you work,
no matter how much this means to you,
sometimes you just lose.

"I love teaching, I love my students, but every teacher knows sometimes kids ask the stupidest questions ever. *'How do I stop a bad guy from punching me if my arms are tied behind my back and I'm blindfolded?'* Do a backflip. *'If the bad guy has seven friends what should I do?'* Use your psychic powers to take them out. *'What if someone tries to stab me while I'm sleeping?'* I'm concerned that you even asked that. *'What if I finish the move, but then I am bleeding really bad; what should I do?'* Go to the hospital. If you're bleeding, you go to the hospital. Did your parents teach you nothing?

Sometimes the answer is don't ask the question. Don't let yourself get to the point where you've already lost."

CONCUSSION

This concussion has me hearing percussion,
I'm seeing double, and I know you're trouble.
Knocked to the floor, I'm floating in the sky,
seeing stars all around, ready to stand and fall.
Concussed and unsure of what I said,
I lied to you, ready to cry but I'm mentally unwell,
emotionally scarred, my brain awake but asleep.
I feel okay, but my eyes are bloodshot and wobbly.
I'm alive, the doctors think I'm dying, well I'm here,
but not presently, I'm walking forward, but every
step is regression. I think I'm making progression,
though my head is aching, every memory failing me.
This concussion has me facing the repercussions
of leaving you out of sight, you started a fight.
I dropped to the ground; I think what I found
is what I lost when I fell to the floor.
A temporary injury has lasting consequences,
this dread and unsurity is a lasting part of me.
I lie down, I lied and found, breaking promises,
taking my past to the breaking point,
breaking my head open, a pathetic excuse
for what is now the paranoia of a recluse.
This concussion has me thinking I'm fine,
but when I start walking, I fall down and
the leaving memories leave a stain of pain.

GOODBYES SUCK

Why do people have to change?
They grow up and decide they
don't want to be your friend anymore.
Then they leave.
They have their new friends,
their new hobbies, their new flirts,
and they don't have me.
It's a new season with a new cast.
I hope this one lasts.
But typically it doesn't, and when they leave,
they don't say goodbye.
Which just might be better.
Let the memory fade away like they did.
But now when I look through old picture books,
I see you again and have to say goodbye on my own.

I need to punch something.

FRIDAY MORNING

When you're sad, punch something.
Preferably not a wall.
When it's Friday morning,
and you're feeling Monday blues,
go and punch something.
I'll scream and cry,
beat up the punching bag till noon.
I don't need gloves.
I'll just let my knuckles bleed.
Let it all out.
Admit defeat.
Punching is a requirement of self-defense.
Punch the bad guy's face to stay safe.
Punch a bag, to remind yourself life will be okay.
Even if right now all you
want to do is scream and cry.
Punch the punching bag,
and take a moment to breathe.
You'll be okay.
It's just another day.

BLOOD, SWEAT, TEARS
A ROCK ANTHEM SONG BY JOSHUA CROCKER

Why is life like this?
Things can be so tough.
I'm just trying to make it another day.
Babe, when I'm at my strongest,
I just feel weak.

Oh, I'm trying!
Trying every day.
I just keep saying,
life can still be great.
Even if I'm crying, dying,
all these challenges in my way.
I know I'll keep fighting
through my fears.
I'll keep fighting
with blood, sweat, 'n' tears.
Oh, I'll keep fighting
with blood, sweat, 'n' tears.

Every trial is trying.
And when opportunity knocks
it's with an obstacle course.
I jump, I leap, I fall flat at that.
Go splat!
Oh why is that?
Why can't things just go my way?
And why do we work so hard for nothing?
I'm trying, I really am.
But anxiety leaves me bloodied.

Oh, I'm trying!
Trying every day.
I just keep saying,
life can still be great.
Even if I'm crying, dying,
all these challenges in my way.
I know I'll keep fighting
through my fears.
I'll keep fighting
with blood, sweat, 'n' tears.
Oh, I'll keep fighting
with blood, sweat, 'n' tears.

Oh! Bloodied and bruised.
Keep going till you collapse.
Crying at the better and worse.

I give absolutely everything,
but I still feel like I left something,
when I have nothing left.
They say it takes pain
for good things to happen,
so if I want to earn this,
if I want anything good, if I want to be good,
then it'll hurt along the way.
It's only because of something bad,
that I can be glad. Isn't that mad?
I'm trying, I really am.
I haven't sweat enough if I'm not the best.

Oh, I'm trying!
Trying every day.
I just keep saying,
life can still be great.
Even if I'm crying, dying,
all these challenges in my way.
I know I'll keep fighting
through my fears.
I'll keep fighting
with blood, sweat, 'n' tears.
Oh, I'll keep fighting
with blood, sweat, 'n' tears.

Oh! Bloodied and bruised.
Keep going till you collapse.
Crying at the better and worse.

Every fight is another knife strike.
Does everything have to be tough?
I know that's just nonsense and fluff,
but it feels like it's right, because it's a fight.
And for every trial and failure, I won't give up.
I'll wear my heart on my sleeve and keep trying.
Because what else can I do but try.
I really am trying.
And these tears are worth it.
They're memories of the happy and sad times.

Oh, I'm trying!
Trying every day.
I just keep saying,
life can still be great.
Even if I'm crying, dying,
all these challenges in my way.
I know I'll keep fighting
through my fears.
I'll keep fighting
with blood, sweat, 'n' tears.
Oh, I'll keep fighting
with blood, sweat, 'n' tears.
I'll keep fighting
with blood, sweat, 'n' tears.
Fight with your heart.
I'll keep fighting
with blood, sweat, 'n' tears.
I'll fight with my heart.

WHAT DO YOU SAY

What do you say to the girl who says, "I love you,"
when you know you don't love her back?
Do you lie or run away?

What do you say to the friend who wants to die?
Do you just spout the same script
they've heard countless times?
"The world needs you. You just need to learn
to love yourself the way I love you."
Does that ever work?

What do you say to the people who hate your friends?
Love the sinner, hate the sin. Whatever.
They've admitted to me love isn't okay anyway.
Can you tolerate intolerance?

What do you say in your prayers at night?
Thank you? Guide me? Keep me safe, please?
I want to make a difference, be the light,
but I don't know which path to take is right.
Can your mind be tongue-tied?

What do you say when you don't know what to say?

IDK

Is everything going to be okay?
Will this move keep me 100% safe?
Can you make me a great martial artist?
I don't know.
But we can learn together.
We'll keep training, growing stronger.
It's okay to say, "I don't know,"
when you haven't got a clue.
Don't give an answer unless you know it's right.
Always take the time to learn and grow.

What is the best kick?
Is Santa Ninja real?
Are you a sensei?
I don't know.
I wish I did, but I'm not Superman.
I'm just a kid. I'm only a black belt.
We're still learning like the rest of you.
It's okay to say, "I don't know."
We'll figure it out together.

Is the world getting better or worse?
I don't know.
Let's figure it out.
We'll make sure the answer is the right one.

AFRAID

I'm afraid.
I'm afraid of everything.
Car crashes, bombs, plague, guns.
Funerals, lying, fire, floods, dying.
I'm afraid of tornados and hail,
I'm afraid of hugging you.
What I say to you is a lie,
I tell you to be brave, stand up for yourself,
but it's all a façade. I'm afraid of it all.

If I hide, if I lie, I can pretend I'm safe.
I'm not. I'm still afraid, afraid of everything.
Theft, recession, pollution, depression.
Existential quandary, am I living a lie?
I'm afraid.
I'm not as brave as you think.

I'm afraid of love, afraid of you and I.
Afraid I care more about people
than they care about me.
I'm afraid.
I'm afraid of everything.
I'm afraid. Afraid. Why?
Will I be okay? Maybe. Maybe not.
Will you be okay? I hope so.
Please be okay.

I'm afraid.
I'm afraid of everything.
Car crashes, bombs, plague, guns.
Funerals, lying, fire, floods, dying.
Tornados, hail, hugging you.
Theft, recession, pollution, depression.
Existential quandary, am I living a lie?
Love, falling in love, you and I, heartbreak.
I'm afraid.
Why?

Af-afraid. Why am I so afraid? Afraid of everything.
I'm still here, I'm still walking, I haven't given up.
So why am I afraid of the things I can't control?
The storms of life, the tragedies of time,
the love story that's not mine.
If anything bad happens at all I'm the one to blame.
Maybe if I was better at life I wouldn't be so afraid.
Or maybe if I wasn't so afraid of being a failure,
I might be brave enough to see all the good in me.

I'm afraid. Afraid of everything.
But I'm still here. I keep fighting back.
Maybe I am as brave as you think.
Every day you and I look fear in the eye,
but we keep going anyway.
I'm afraid. Are you afraid?
We're still here.
I'm afraid that makes us all the braver.

"I learned that courage was not the absence of fear, but the triumph over it. The brave man is not he who does not feel afraid, but he who conquers that fear."

-   *Nelson Mandela*

HEY LITTLE ONE
TAKEN FROM SNIPPETS OF INK

Hey little one,
some days it takes courage just to get out of bed
when blankets give more warmth than the world.
Remember, you don't need to slay a dragon
to have an adventure.
It takes confidence just to walk outside.

Hey little one,
some days it takes courage just to smile
when you have doubts about what you're doing.
Remember, you don't need to live a story tale
to find a little joy.
It takes confidence just to be able to feel sad.

Hey little one,
some days it takes courage just to be you.
But we all love it when you do.

EVERYDAY HEROES

The world needs you to be amazing.
I get it, things are scary.
But you gotta put on your cape,
go ahead and wear your smile,
and be an everyday hero.

Be a leader in the community,
be a friend at school,
be a hero in the world.
You don't have to fly to save today,
hold the door open for the person with full hands,
encourage your friends, speak kindly,
pick up litter, stand up for what's right,
share and give, think considerately of others.
Things are scary. There's sadness everywhere.
The world needs you to be amazing.
Be a leader even in a small way.
Be a hero every day.

FIGHT BACK

One of the biggest lessons I've learned in my time doing karate is to fight back. With a kick, jab, cross, you'll close the gap. You'll take them down to the ground. You'll stand back up and run away. You'll stand up for what you believe in. C'mon, we got this.

One of the hardest things I've come to realize is it's okay to not be perfect. Not every kick will land. But when my foot hits the ground instead of your head, I'll just throw a punch next. I'll keep fighting. I'm going to keep writing, and keep up the rhyming, and let the flame keep igniting.

One of the toughest things to do is be human. To feel pain on the outside and even more so on the inside. To keep trying to grow as a person, to become a better one every day. I'm a black belt. Not because I won a fight once five years ago. But because every day I fight back.

This book is filled with my stories, my words. Do with them what you will. I wrote it for the kids, who just like me, want to fight back.
C'mon, we got this.

READ THIS

Why can't I comprehend that I'm not
going to win an award every day?
Seemingly, every day needs to be a movie,
but the special effects budget is running dry.
Not every word is a song
and not every second is special.

Oh, love feels like a punch to the face,
a kick between the legs,
and every time I try to throw a block
I forget to evade to the side.

Every book still on the shelf, not sold.
Every page on my coffee table, not opened.
Every training day spent on the couch.
Every string I'm afraid is too good to be strung.
Every prayer left unsaid.
Every friend I left on read.
Every second gone by, a second not mine.

Oh, love feels like a punch to the face,
a kick between the legs,
and every time I try to throw a block
I forget to evade to the side.

If you can't love yourself, they say,
why do you think you can love anyone else?
If you can't slip a punch,
don't wonder why there is blood on your nose.
The world is so big,
but my mind so small.
I can't grasp or think,
if I can't retreat.

Oh, love feels like a punch to the face,
a kick between the legs,
and every time I try to throw a block
I forget to evade to the side.

Read this, my love.
And remember. The sun will set. And rise again.
Stop running when you can walk.
Stop blocking when you can punch.
Write and read. Don't click and click.
You can't stay in your head
typing a script for every day,
when every conversation is improv,
every match is freestyle fighting,
and love is better spent.

317 -- SELF-DEFENSE CLASS

GRAPPLING DISTANCE

I'm stuck in grappling distance.
I'm fighting for a clinch.
I'm afraid to be taken down.

If I let someone close,
I have to let my guard down.
And I'm scared that will make me weak.

I don't need anyone else.
I'm a kicker. I want you to stay away.
Don't grab hold of me.

But when life punches you in the face,
who's going to help pick you up from the floor?
Who's going to let their guard down,
and give you a hug?

I'm stuck in grappling distance.
I want to elbow away, pull back to kicking range.
But sometimes you have to get close to someone,
be honest with them, trust them, love them,
and let them hug you when you feel down.

CRY THE WORLD

Cry the world away.
When you take a beating,
don't stop breathing.
Oh, cry the world away.

Are you bleeding?
When you take a punch,
breathe in and out.
Stand up.
Don't quit fighting,
just cause you got hurt once.

Cry the world away.
Let your guard down.
Only when you're vulnerable,
will you grow stronger.
Oh, cry the world away.

Self-defense isn't magic.
It's realistic.
This is a class on self-defense.
There will be tears along the way.
I'll admit it, you're going to get hit.
Bruises and scars await you.
But when you cry the world away,
you'll realize the strength will always stay.

I WANT TO FIGHT

"Mr. Joshua, it's because I want to fight," says Finley.
I turn and look at my student next to me.
"You want to fight? Like right now?" I seem puzzled.
"No, the answer to your question is, 'I want to fight.'"
"What." I respond.
"I have no clue what you're talking about."
"Remember? You asked me why I do martial arts."
I look at Finley.
The only thing I said to them today was hello.
"When did I ask you that?"
Finley starts getting annoyed with me,
"Remember when I was having that bad class a few
months ago. You asked me why I do martial arts.
Ever since I've been trying to figure out the answer.
And I finally figured it. I want to learn to fight."

Oh, yeah.
I finally remember what they're talking about.
"I'm glad you figured out what your 'why' is.
I am a little concerned about your answer though."
Finley explains, "Well, I was thinking about what
makes self-defense important. And it's to stay safe,
right? And sometimes you have to fight to stay safe."
"Absolutely. I guess that's a good answer."

I start to walk away to finish what I was doing,
but Finley keep following after me.
They say, "But then I thought about it more.
You have to always keep fighting.
It's like you told me, never give up. You'll never
get better at the things you love if you quit.
And then one day in class I realized that you
can find a way to succeed, even in smaller ways.
It made me think of all the things
that were important to me,
and I realized that's sorta what
self-defense is all about.
You have to fight for the things
that are important to you. And to me,
learning martial arts is important,
so I want to keep fighting and keep getting better.
Even if sometimes I don't succeed right away
or I get hit, I'll keep fighting."

I pause. I smile.
"I never could have given an answer that good.
And I can't think of a better reason
why to learn self-defense."

"Do you get it yet? There is more to a self-defense class than punching. Please listen to me. If you want to stay safe you have to protect yourself. You just have to. The world isn't getting any better. That's just how it works; things have been awful since the beginning. But we've also had love this whole time. We've had a hope building in us.

Self-defense is exactly that. Defense against the self. All those thoughts, all the despair inside. You can be a world class fighter. But that doesn't make you safe. Safety is an illusion. Confidence is faith, not a certainty. To love is a choice. So make the choice every day to love others, you can make the world a better place. Make the choice to love yourself. And just know, there's no better self-defense than that."

QUESTION

"Any questions?" I say.
A student raises their hand.
They ask, "What is the best move for self-defense?"
I smile. "Be aware. Fight back.
Look out for everyone. Love everyone.
That includes you."

Index

Songs

12 Days of Kick-mas	pg. 199-204
Blood, Sweat, Tears	pg. 301-304
Chi Power	pg. 19-22
Growing Up Is Hard	pg. 240-244
The Hero With No Powers	pg. 181-184
Kick Like a Girl	pg. 104-107
Kick-mas Miracle	pg. 217-220
Loud	pg. 67-70
Music About Punching People	pg. 6-8
Nostalgia Is In the Journey	pg. 255-257
One More Step	pg. 47-50
Purple Gi	pg. 35-38
Traditional Dojo	pg. 135-138
What She Was Told	pg. 281-285
You Don't Say	pg. 120-122

Poems

4 Ways	pg. 46
Afraid	pg. 307-308
All the Basic Releases	pg. 40
All the Same	pg. 74
Americana	pg. 58
Apologize	pg. 187
Become the Best	pg. 176

Beginner's Mind	pg. 169
The Best Style	pg. 73
Black Belt	pg. 292-293
Black Belt Body	pg. 170
Blue Belt	pg. 223
Brown Belt	pg. 270
Bubble	pg. 287
Bully Defense	pg. 238
Bunkbed Bunkai	pg. 251
Butterflies	pg. 102
Caroling In the Living Room	pg. 209
Child Prodigy	pg. 250
Concussion	pg. 298
Crane Kick I	pg. 87
Crane Kick II	pg. 88
Cry the World	pg. 319
Don't Be Stupid	pg. 65
Don't Forget to Be Awesome	pg. 18
Don't Say a Thing	pg. 188
Don't Tell Me What I'm Not	pg. 133
Dress Up	pg. 178
Drop the Beat	pg. 72
Earn Respect	pg. 157
Everyday Heroes	pg. 312
Everyone	pg. 2-3
Favorite Word	pg. 119
Fight Back	pg. 313
Fight to Fight Another Day	pg. 64

Fighting, Fighting; Same, Same	pg. 271-272
The First Class I Taught	pg. 115
Four Parts	pg. 83
Freakin' Great	pg. 118
The French Revolution	pg. 57
Friday Morning	pg. 300
Get Ready	pg. 13
Goodbyes Suck	pg. 299
Grappling Range	pg. 318
The Grappling Rule	pg. 41
Green Belt	pg. 145
Grow With Your Peers	pg. 160
Hands Up	pg. 76
The Havendry Family	pg. 139-140
Hey Little One	pg. 310
I Want to Fight	pg. 321-322
I Will Succeed	pg. 164
IDK	pg. 306
I'm Not the Hero	pg. 191
I'm the Cooler Karate Kid	pg. 274-275
I'm the Hero / I Can Save You	pg. 179-180
Instruction Manual: Axe Kick	pg. 90
Instruction Manual: Back Kick	pg. 85
Instruction Manual: Crecent Kick	pg. 89
Instruction Manual: Front Kick	pg. 78
Instruction Manual: Hook Kick	pg. 96
Instruction Manual: Round Kick	pg. 81
Instruction Manual: Side Kick	pg. 80

Instruction Manual: Twist Kick   pg. 97
Invest In Yourself   pg. 152
Jab, Cross   pg. 43
Jingle   pg. 205
Kata Memorization 101   pg. 54
A Knight's Adventure   pg. 55
Last One Standing   pg. 185
Lightbulb Moment   pg. 131
Little Kids   pg. 129
A Long and Convoluted Story   pg. 261-266
Lose, Lose   pg. 295
Making a Living Kicking   pg. 125
Mats   pg. 15
Mental Health, Self-Defense   pg. 279
A Musical Extravaganza   pg. 224-228
My Sidekick   pg. 61
Never Give Up   pg. 153
A Nun With a Nunchuck   pg. 23
Onward and Up   pg. 207-208
Orange Belt   pg. 98
Paiosamu Kata   pg. 215-216
Play Guitar In Gi   pg. 4
Portrait   pg. 132
Printer   pg. 114
Punching Poem   pg. 75
Purple Belt   pg. 175
Question   pg. 324
Reach Your Goals   pg. 161

Read This   pg. 315-316
Roll With the Punches   pg. 9-11
Santa Ninja   pg. 212
Scraped Knee   pg. 16
Smile   pg. 44
Snowy Field   pg. 210
So, You Know Karate?   pg. 28
Soccer and Football   pg. 235
Stand Up   pg. 267
Sticker Line   pg. 237
Still Doing Karate   pg. 259
Stockings   pg. 196
Strikeout   pg. 60
Student and Teacher   pg. 150
Success   pg. 147
Teach By Example   pg. 156
Test Your Limits   pg. 139
Testing Night   pg. 32
That Holiday Feeling   pg. 222
Thirteen and Counting   pg. 233
Throwing Star   pg. 25
Thunderous I   pg. 84
Thunderous II   pg. 91
Thunderous III   pg. 100
Thunderous IV   pg. 109-110
Time Well Spent   pg. 127
Training   pg. 29
Trampoline   pg. 93

Try and Stop Me   pg. 146
'Twas the Night   pg. 197
Validity   pg. 289
Violence I   pg. 142
Violence II   pg. 143
Virtual Learning   pg. 254
Warning: Don't Touch   pg. 288
Warrior's Heart   pg. 171
The Way of the Samurai   pg. 174
The Way of the Samurai II   pg. 194
What Do You Say   pg. 305
What Do You Want to Be   pg. 234
What Is the Best Kick?   pg. 112
What's Your Why?   pg. 33-34
When I Actually Started Teaching   pg. 116
White Belt   pg. 12
Will You Focus!   pg. 236
A Winter Letter   pg. 229-230
Yeah, I'd Say I'm Pretty Tough   pg. 248
Yellow Belt   pg. 52
Yes I Can!   pg. 168
You've Got This   pg. 246

331 -- JOSHUA CROCKER

Acknowledgments

In March 2023 I was sitting in at my computer, writing. I had about an hour before I needed to be at work for a private lesson. As I was reading over something I wrote, I had an idea. I wanted to write a book for my students; for people who love martial arts. So as I wrote this book, I had my students in mind. I am so grateful to have the opportunity to teach you all martial arts and I hope the songs and stories spoke to you. Keep training! Each one of you are awesome.

I've been training in the martial arts for over a decade, and I couldn't have done it without my family and friends. I love training, but you all are what makes it special. So to each one of you, thank you and know that we all need a team behind us. I look forward to kicking you all for years to come.

With love to everyone at Integrity Martial Arts, my dojo. Thank you all for the chance to learn and teach. And a special thank you to the black belt family at Integrity, who make the dojo the special place it is. We are a family not because we are all black belts, but because of the years spent on the mats training together. Thank you to Alex, Brian, Bridgette, Dan, Debra, Eric, Greg, John, Jonathan, Kevin, Luke, Phil, and Samantha.

333 -- JOSHUA CROCKER

About Joshua

Joshua Crocker lives in Norman, OK. He works for Integrity Martial Arts as an instructor and media lead. He earned his black belt in September 2018 (and his junior black belt two years prior). He trains primarily in Tae Kwon Do, Isshinryu Karate, Brazilian Jiu-Jitsu, and Kickboxing. Joshua started teaching classes in 2021 and is now a full-time martial arts instructor. He heads the leadership team at his dojo, aiming to inspire a team of future leaders both on and off the mats.

Joshua started training in 2010 when he was six-years-old. Shortly after, his mom and sister joined him on the mats, and they have been training together ever since. His mom is a co-owner of Integrity Martial Arts and the two work closely together. Joshua's brother started training when he turned four and is now one of the students in their dojo's leadership team. Joshua's step-dad is one of his martial arts teachers and a huge influence on his growth as a martial artist and teacher. The two have a podcast together, *Kicking for a Living*, about martial arts and business.

Joshua has written two other books: *One Day I'll Know* and *Snippets of Ink*. He's hard at work on an exciting slate of future literary projects. Joshua has also been expanding his skills in video editing and documentary filming. And if he ever gets good enough at singing and playing guitar, he promises to teach a whole class as a musical, with the occasional joke thrown in.

www.ingramcontent.com/pod-product-compliance
Lightning Source LLC
Chambersburg PA
CBHW030356130626
46549CB00004B/1515